ZEKE'S GUIDE TO TRAVEL & LIFE: MEXICO

STORIES FROM THE ROAD AND ALL
YOU NEED TO KNOW TO EMBARK ON
YOUR OWN ADVENTURE TRAVELS

CHARLES BOWDEN

Copyrighted Material

Zeke's Guide to Travel & Life
Copyright © 2021 by by Charles Bowden. All Rights Reserved.
No part of this publication may be reproduced, stored in a retrieval system or transmitted, in any form or by any means—electronic, mechanical, photocopying, recording or otherwise—without prior written permission from the publisher, except for the inclusion of brief quotations in a review.

For information about this title or to order other books and/or electronic media, contact the publisher:
Beauty Spot Press
chrlsbwdn46@gmail.com

Library of Congress Control Number: 2019919720

ISBN: 978-1-7341483-0-5 (softcover)
        978-1-7341483-1-2 (ebook)

Printed in the United States of America
Cover and Interior design: 1106 Design

For Joan and Indy

By the same author

Zeke's Guide to Travel and Life:

Volume 2: CHINA/TIBET

Volume 3: TURKEY—EGYPT—ISRAEL/PALESTINE *(coming soon)*

Volume 4: INDIA—PAKISTAN—UZBEKISTAN—RUSSIA *(coming soon)*

PRELUDE

It began with a series of desperate situations. In the course of which, it entered Zeke's mind to routinely self-program in such a way as to stay alive and keep going. Although, doing that unfolded only gradually, and only as a pattern, not a default mode. For he lived in those wayward days when computers were only entering upon their first bloom—long before the robots seized power. All Zeke's primitive procedures for self-preservation through self-command had for tools were an erasable pen, paper, and his own faulty memory.

On the earth below, he saw a faint trail go left into a dry, narrow gully. At first seemingly the trail shown on his map, going on down to the road. Soon, though, all boot prints in its sand gave out, and he descended a succession of low bedrock ledges. And as he went along, round each bend, the step down got larger. Also, the dry gulch's walls got taller,

Prelude

but never mind that. Although his worn bypath was harder to see now, he still reckoned that way for a shortcut.

It's a mistake to shortcut California's Big Sur coast. Redwood groves in ravines. Live oak. Green grass in uplifted sea meadows. Bunches of gloriously invasive pampas grass, with beige-white feathery plumes above the bounding main. Aquamarine, it plays, with patches of ochre kelp beneath the shoal water. Mountain tops become islands above coastal fog. The gulch was pale limestone, crusted terra cotta, like a layer of rust. These were only some of the coast's more obvious charms.

Meanwhile, his gully, turned ravine, was bearing about where the compass said it should. Only he could never see for sure that it went all the way—that's what you get walking down slope through a ravine. So, on tired legs, he tried to figure things out. Taking another glance at the map, it now led him to believe that he was trudging a dry Lime Kiln Creek toward the coast. What do maps know of shortcuts, though? Here a creek had turned into a de facto trail.

He kept going down. When round a bend there came a boulder stair so high that he had to lower his backpack on rope before facing the barrier and cautiously balancing his way down. Then, beyond the next bend, was a bigger drop that he descended in the same manner. But Zeke was bushed from all this scrambling after a long day's hike. His head, attached as it was, ultimately, to his legs and feet, lacked its standard amount of energy, too. Consequently, a determination to stop and turn back hadn't quite gained a foothold against the sentiment that clambering way back up would be too much work by then.

Prelude

Only on the verge of what looked to be a 50-foot drop-off, with rocks at the bottom, did he give up on it. A big waterfall during rains. He hadn't enough rope, strength, climbing skill, or pure, stupid courage to give it a shot. The end of the non-trail, it was. Where, at that extremity, standing on the brink, *it* then slipped into his consciousness—that whisper of panic behind a doubt that going back up the way he came was feasible. Was it? Not with the burden of a full pack, it wasn't.

Back up there with gravity on his side, a few times he had lowered his pack by rope. Down plunging rock faces where its heaviness discouraged wearing it. Now, since formations projected at odd angles in these places, neither strength nor elbow room would allow drawing upwards the same mass on a rope. Zeke was skinny. Even with solid footing, his thin arms and slim back wouldn't overcome that much drag of friction and gravity. Between right-angled ravine sides, he'd been caught unawares, like a rodent in a cage trap with one-way doors!

Fear was a hot tingling sensation in his shoulders, neck, and upper chest. He stiffened. Stepping back from the edge, he staggered, under the distraction of a surging self-pity. Then came a few tears, fitful breathing, and a weight in his belly—all tied in with the notion that the world was way out of control and might soon destroy him.

He shut it out for the time being, closing his eyes. The next thing he saw was a rock in the wall he was fronting, back from the rim. A tangible item to remind him that he was solidly alive, so far. So he turned his close attention inward to his out-of-control emotionalism—in the same ominous state as

Prelude

the world about it. Well, homing in on that, after the rock, gave the signal to grasp immediate reality and to hold down morbid presuppositions about a severely limited future—to squash his agitation by decidedly noticing it. Hearing himself fall apart, burst out crying, would be counterproductive, he realized, demoralizing. Hopeless weeping and panic would block escape. When anxiety descends into fear, concentration falls off. So he sat down, to wait for his feelings to settle. After a moment, he was finally able to focus on the here-and-now. He began trying to think of a way out of his predicament.

Were he a more seasoned backpacker in those days, his unseemly woe might have suggested a strategic night's sleep before attempting an escape. His tired muscles *did* make rest tempting, even so. But his arroyo bed was covered with sharp, embedded rocks where it wasn't angled down overmuch. Thoroughly uncomfortable, with no way he knew of to stake a tent. And what if it rained hard after dark? *Whoosh!* Flash-flooded into oblivion; his last nightmare of a spider down a rainspout.

Think! First off, leaving behind his heavy pack and climbing *up* for more rope was an extremely unappealing plan. It was late afternoon. Blackness and the danger of hypothermia were approaching. And what were his chances of coming upon a helpful hiker with plenty of rope up there? National Forest trails thereabouts saw fewer hikers in those days. Besides, scrambling up and then back down with rope would up his chances of taking a tumble in these out-of-reach whereabouts. Moreover, given enough hypothetical rope, the doubtfulness of him winging a rappel *down* one or more precipices was too

Prelude

big. He'd never rappelled and couldn't even visualize how the rope should fasten about him.

The remaining possibility was a new way up. But the ravine walls were steep and about as tall as a two- or three-story building on both sides. Greenish-gray to terra cotta, the crumbly shale and yielding gritty soil that was held up only by thick, limey, dried mud and pebbles. Though here and there larger rocks protruded from this unstable natural stucco, the ravine walls were almost straight up and down. And yet, and yet... the longer he kept his eyes upon one of them, the more climbable it seemed.

After roughly picking out a route, he decided to just give it a try. Contributing were both mental fatigue and a phobic fret—trapped in a deep grave! Being too green at climbing to reckon from below how excessively vertical a steep slope may turn out up above did as well. He strapped back on his hefty pack and started up.

Zeke was facing a soft-enough crust for kicking shallow toeholds, but one remarkably vertical for what little rock showed. And as it stretched upward, its slant got worse and his undertaking more precarious. Nonetheless, by clawing fingerholds for balance and booting toeholds, he gingerly eased upward—or sideways—for minor improvements in his angle of body tilt. Stones came loose in his hands. He constantly tested them first. And as he persevered, his clinging body burned adrenalin, but no strain registered. He was fighting for life.

His mind was lucid, but there was something odd about it—as if autopilot were taking over. A firmness from out beyond his close-up intentness was directing each motion he made.

Prelude

His limbs were responding to brief commands from a captain somewhere. About all Zeke's own familiar prod of wording accomplished was a repetitive "Purchase . . . Purchase . . . Purchase . . ." Which self-urging, broadly, to find purchase only punctuated the intervals dividing his captain's express orders.

"Left toe way over there. Dig it in more. Now test it. Dig in your fingers. Cautiously shift your weight . . .", and so on. A strangely calm voice had taken over his stream of consciousness. Itself barely identifiable now as his own. And there was the further oddity that his frequent daydreams of previous times and localities had all quit. As if his tomorrow was then too uncertain for any yesterdays to raise concern. He was right there, and nowhere else. Once or twice, though, during respites, he muttered for his own benefit: "I *do* want to go on living."

After a dreadful while, he made it to a thin upper edge: an unstable ridge line with eroded gaps and with cliffs both sides. After a rest, he did a balancing act back along it, edging up to the trail above. With the worst part over, "Purchase!" shifted from thought to speech. He said that word every few minutes, to prompt alertness. Crossing a jagged section, after one boot slid, Zeke, in a rational tone said even more: "You're obviously going too fast. Slow down, idiot!"

By then it was only he, out alone, giving himself orders, in one of his accustomed forms of self-address, thinking aloud for emphasis. The *captain's* specific orders had only been lucid *thoughts*. "Don't try saving time while out on this," Zeke soliloquized, although dusk was settling. When he'd been clawing his way up the wall, there had been someone else's

Prelude

voice in his skull! Now Zeke was only impersonating that Captain Courageous. Along with his directive utterances now came comments, taunts, and inessential mention of his overall location. He was no longer receiving them from high command.

The first level site by the trail after he came out, and up went his tent. And he was as joyful as he possibly could be, considering his exhaustion. "Tenuous! Tenuous escape!" Two more words with strong "-s" aspirations, like the beginning of "sleep," were now uppermost. Before slumber came, he promised "not to forget this day without learning from it."

On his way down next morning, out of Los Padres National Forest, Zeke was pleased. Then, gaining California Highway 1 made him happy. There was scant traffic to hitchhike in his direction, though. So his smile accomplished nothing by way of roving south; he was out of luck. Before long, two men rounded a curve uphill and strolled down. (It was the '60s; before that road got busy and unsafe for exercise walkers and maybe cars, too—certainly for cars pulling trailers or mobile homes. Before the day wise guys were saying that it should be converted to a bicycle path.)

Pleasantries were exchanged. Soon, the smooth-spoken one, with all the presence of a California guru or crack psychotherapist, asked Zeke why he was hitchhiking and not driving a car of his own. Zeke flung off that he didn't want a car much. "Why not?" "I feel I'll go farther in life without one" was his cryptic reply. It came out of his mouth spontaneously. Was it just then he was glad enough to yet have legs?

Prelude

Without hesitation, confidently, the man assured Zeke that he was "on the road to wisdom." Exact words.

Zeke would remember this chance encounter. The gentleman, much his senior, was plausibly only someone from the close Esalen Institute, out for a walk with his disciple or student. But in looking back, this transient meeting took on heavy significance. As if he had gone into the forest on a solitary vision quest but then, in coming away, received a waking inner-transformation message from a Jungian archetype. (The therapist: symbolizing sanity?) Or as if, soon after a close scrape with death, he'd had a cursory soul-search by an angel. It was then, after that event, that he began programming himself to use his term on Earth effectively and safely—enough to go far.

To get along, Zeke easily kept smiling by the road. Below which smile dangled a skinny youth with a ridiculously elongated neck. That would be him, looking like he'd run off from the circus. But as a hitchhiker of long standing, he came to trust that his scrawniness, along with his boyish features, helped get rides. Further, he was given to understand that having an extreme sort of physique also helps an introspective journey. (From another sage on another road who once gave a ride: "Your soul, not travel, is your real trip. But you know that...")

Zeke's soul came in a freaky package: shoulders so narrow, a chest so flat, and legs so long as to remind you of a fat-headed Giacometti figure. His lankiness made his noggin seem large, so that when he tilted it forward in nodding agreement, it might look ready to topple off his thin neck. So, how

Prelude

would everybody react to such a frail specimen of manhood? With indifference mostly. He was unpopular enough in high school, more so from there on out. By which he was taught a certain standoffishness even from himself.

But did he have what it takes to be a vagabond? Definitely, he did. Since attachments were few and far between, there was little to stop him drifting. Which he felt like doing from early on. Thumbing rides, mostly in New England, started after his first hometown college stint and then continued back and forth to the West Coast. After transferring to a university elsewhere, he rode the rails a couple times cross-country but soon returned to interstate on-ramps. Cars were cleaner and more comfortable.

Then, one time en route to California, he ventured upon a long walk in Colorado National Monument. The dusty footpath going by gigantic natural sculptures, in seclusion and tranquility, in terrain so different from where he'd come of age. It made him burst out laughing! He was enjoying a holiday from all his youthful difficulties. After that day, hiking came to be his preferred way of getting ahead and getting a life.

He met few others on that trail and on the ones he began frequently walking after it. Which gave him a new theory about population density and stress. That self-consciousness out in public—awareness of looking bad to others in any way—sets in motion regretful memories which, in turn, are the primary source of occasional depression. On-the-spot regret collects and energizes sorrowful memories. Therefore, the external factor that most inhibits happiness during a journey is population pressure—the stress of that does.

Prelude

Fewest cues to feel regret occur on a wilderness trail, or even along a little-used dirt road or country path. The second-most psychologically favorable setting occurs living on the edge of wilderness, near a grocery store or restaurant. (Maybe during rainy periods in your tent.) The third-most psychologically favorable environments are routes taken outside wilderness areas, in all types of vehicles, to and from towns or settlements, through the countryside. And, of course, the environments most inimical to joy would be urban or suburban ones. Which tend to have more ill effect upon your disposition the more population density they have.

Boy Zeke's hometown in Pennsylvania was small. Grovers Corners. In and close to it lay a river, a college campus, a swamp, railroad tracks, and a hilly tangle of country roads. Nostalgia for childhood invested the campus lawns, ivied halls, rhododendron bushes, the sensuous and solemn organ vibrations of distant train whistles, cycling way out of town on back roads, a leaky rowboat on lazy Wolf Creek above the dam, bounding over scattered tussocks and humps of higher ground keep from wet feet in the swamp, the sledding hill with bumps at the bottom, his grandparents' farm, and the delicate odor of the wildwoods. Back then, nobody knew how passionately Zeke yearned to explore new territory. Many kids or youths go through that phase but then grow out of it. He was off-center that way, for keeps.

Zeke grew into a bookish nerd who blew tenor saxophone none too well. Nevertheless, before graduation, a girl in his high school band hinted marriage—a second woodwind who tittered at his jokes—but he had other intentions. Shyly, he squirmed out of her clutches. He wanted more experiences first. Which for him, principally referred to satisfied wanderlust. But that friendly clarinetist was the first society almost had him.

Instead of the lonely existence he embarked upon, conceivably, he should have watched for and then taken wing with that rare bird, a drifting girlfriend. But he hadn't the confidence or wherewithal. Also, few women welcomed his company, by any means, due both to his looks and mousiness. Stemming from which were one or two decades when many urbanites of California and other states, on sight, were leery of his sexual orientation. Zeke conceded this impression only after indelible incidents made it seem more than likely. Somewhat later, though, when the question of his straightness had lost most of its zing, he was positive.

Once he saw a program on television in which a group from a Hollywood audience, both genders and a few races, were doing their level best to guess which male in successive lineups of six on stage was gay. The stationary men introduced themselves briefly, yet notions about them were necessarily based more upon their surface appearance and way of saying than their words or motions. A professor who had a hot book on the topic—and did not seem fruity himself—gave the proceedings almost the respectability of a scientific experiment.

Although the audience members were offered generous prizes for picking right, most guessed wrong. The groups of men who, by turns, occupied the spotlight, were all white.

Prelude

Yet, of all those in their mixed audience guessing, the best at it was a black man. (The worst was an Asian man.) The champion queer-spotter explained to the host afterwards that he had chosen mostly on the basis of vocal cues. The others, it emerged, were going more on visual ones. A long neck, good-looking face and hair, nice clothes, and tenseness about the eyes were all cited as convincing details. Also, the more slender specimens usually got most votes.

Thanks to prime-time television, Zeke's worst suspicions were confirmed. He displayed all the telltale signs of how queers look, by the lights of your average studio audience. So, through all his maturity thus far, he hadn't been as paranoid as he feared! Looking back, being stuck in a false cliché about homos was the serious handicap producing a more alienated outlook than burdened many stouter male waders in the muddy waterhole of television. Since what else slants an individual's perspective as much as their looks do? (Short of a stagnant class system or a psychiatric disorder). All the more so when he or she is wholly convinced of being unattractive. It rivals and may revise their natural-born temperament.

There are salient qualities beyond wit or will that determine a person's whole story, their viability. The finger of fate switches on a Brand X human television set that broadcasts, through no choice of the set, a cop show with a queerly thin man in it. The TV script is too short and not clever enough to make possible much in the way of either character or physical development. (With barbells?) So the masculine Twiggy doesn't get much of a part.

Prelude

He may be still more inflexibly cast if, by nature, he is also introverted. Which is why, for bashful old Zeke, there wasn't much on. His traits and looks, assigned by chance at birth, didn't ripen him for stardom. Instead, they constantly gave his transmitted image more or less fuzzy reception. But hold on there! That would sort of contradict Judeo-Christianity, which posits free will (excluding Calvinists). The very whatsit that goes well with ethics.

"Willpower—eat bigger meals and more often!" bellowed a husky heckler from the rear of the studio audience.

"Is he bad-mouthing *me*," wondered Zeke, "or mostly my philosophy?"

He was distrustful of strangers' remarks. His ego was overworked. All in all, he was too susceptible to the personal implications of close happenstance, having a chronic overestimation of how much everyone and everything pointed his way.

Typical of Zeke's category of body structure (ectomorphic) was a liking for going solo. Introversion is known to have a significant genetic base. A propensity that often goes, in males, with extreme lankiness. To bloom (or not) in hidden places, fonder of books than parties, introspective, reserved. It accounted for why Zeke was off on a side path apart at Big Sur, sticking out his long neck way off in backcountry, where no one was apt to hear his cry after a fall from grace. It was his destiny to walk alone and find his own road to follow.

Next day, down the coast, Zeke spilled onto a beach. Very dressed, he sat down on a drift log, peering out to sea and at

Prelude

wavelets on the sand; he was struck by the fact that his capacity had an ebb and flow. At high tide, he felt in possession of his faculties and sometimes capable of sensible thinking. The high surf even enabled him to swim out beyond his day-to-day pragmatic thought-patterns into something or other noteworthy, into body surfing a glittering generality. But those waves dependably swept him back ashore and rolled him onto the sand again.

Mostly, though, he merely lay on the beach, anyhow—along with imaginary others. Social-mindedness, aspiring to wistful, burdened him. He seemed to expend as much brainpower on harassing, semi-coherent bits and pieces of unreal gab and dramatics as on actual person-to-person dialogue, reading, and deep-think all combined. It bothered his sense of efficiency. Stranger yet, he saw that the more steadily he generalized, the more substantial, in turn, his daydreamy interactions with others bulked up. Perhaps, in some way, his stale, self-centered dreaminess ultimately paid for those free, impersonal musings out on the waves. Those surfing curls of brainpower rolling in. As melodramatic wishful thinking may be what a flabby, shaping imagination does for warm-up calisthenics on the shore—or in its energy-saving mode, with no ongoing immersion demanding mindfulness.

All that was off the subject, though. What Zeke actually wanted to think over was how to avoid straying into future life-threatening situations, like his Lime Kiln Creek escapade of yesterday. And already he knew that such know-how would call for sensible thinking at high tide, not comic-book romances on the beach.

Prelude

Reflecting upon his captivity in a one-way gravity mousetrap, he saw it wasn't the first he'd put himself at risk in the out-of-doors. "Some lab assistant should condition me to watch my step in circumstances liable to give grief... No, *me* it has to be." Zeke was his own furry friend, out experimenting, sorting himself out. He should therefore keep track of all misadventures and setbacks, so as not to repeat. Boo-boos tend to repeat. He *must* adapt to that brutal fact. If only he could accurately remember, and infallibly note, how bad his mishaps were, and how they happened. Then he wouldn't be condemned to repeat so many low points in his curious history, to paraphrase Lord Acton. Hard cheese, that, to chew over.

From then on, he began sinking his teeth into his footloose clumsiness more. Until noting on paper his many itinerant wrong moves grew routine. Catching himself in error, chastened, he then wrote down how to correct for what he'd done. From which soon unfurled a dynamic new phase—doing so in the form of directives. A more concise and urgent manner of expression, easier to retain and give high priority. Thus, a heap of pragmatic advice, left behind by his pen pushing, accumulated in the aftermath of Zeke's climbing ordeal at Big Sur. Was his Captain taking the helm for good and all, and Zeke sailing away with him?

One of Zeke's peculiarities was how long and severely he ruminated over his faults, compared with most. He had no patience with himself. Both his recall and anticipation of blunders were overactive. Minor depression was getting flattened from recognizing his ineptitudes in the mirror without knowing how to quit using that greasy kids' stuff and make

Prelude

his hair look great. As well, it came from viewing his awkward interactions, losses, and predicaments as all-pervasive—as more than discrete, impermanent events. Whose repetition might be prevented by appropriate written instructions.

Forsooth, the mistakes of Zeke's red-faced youth caused him two distinct kinds of anguished defeat. First, regret over the consequences in themselves. Second, distress over his very incompetence. Then, if he fluffed new stuff, residual misery from his preceding defeat seeped out like spilled gunpowder. A spark of self-pity, and the both of them blew up out of all proportion. It could ruin his morale.

Originally, indoor scribbling at his desk was mainly first-aid for swollen dissatisfaction with his dumb self down home. Even after getting over most of his desperation there, however, rule-writing lingered on as a hobby to pursue in transit. Wherever he was, how satisfying to run across new patterns among his quirks and then formulate standard operating procedures to give them the slip. Another problem solved! Hypothetically, anyway. To raise your output of error, trip. Furthermore, flopping in new locations gave rise to extra wariness when confronting unfamiliarity. It brought on more practical-mindedness. As he went along, awrong, fresh headway was made. His traveling techniques emerged and then multiplied.

But all-around maxims for flocking, teaming up, or partnering—in the interests of friendship, business, or what-not—proved rough sledding, due to his shyness. Then, too, after their creation, applying these was cumbersome, measured against travel tips, due to subtle intricacies of circumstance and the rapid response times required. For all of that, as an introvert, his enthusiasm for conversation or profit was nowhere near as considerable as the appeal of wandering off to where no one spoke to him much, as when trekking on foreign soil.

"Nothing else whets the mind like a great passion," they slobber over and over. And so it was that making up basic directions for getting around, what he liked most, whether in the woods or at an airport, was what he got into. Practical guidance, culled from his long experience as a globetrotter. His rules of the road directory it became.

SWOOSH! SWOOSH! BARRROOM! Zeke stood beside a freeway on-ramp, just back from where it merged. Edge of a suburb, he was, away from the coastline, in the auto desert of southern California, trying to hook a ride. But his mind went drifting off the road, out of focus, hopelessly stoned. His hostess, after breakfast, generously presented a hashish brownie as he left her back then. Now it was coming on—like a big rig.

"I should have saved it till afterwhile," he was thinking. "Broken it into four servings." (Visions of those very thoughts reverberated before his eyes, printed, in quotation marks, directly after their occurrence, and then oppressively occupied him some before fading out.) "Way out in the woods is where I should be!" he next read on his mind. Then his thinking began mixing sentence fragments with pictures and background noise, too. SWOOSH! SWOOSH! BARRROOM! "What did I just think?" His prior thought-balloon had burst.

They said a bad setting for LSD could bring on bad trips. In kind, from where he stood, by the freeway, it was beginning to seem as though a large dose of hashish out of place could,

Prelude

too. Ominously, diagnosing the why of his predicament did not make it go away.

Soon, he was feeling exposed. Both by the earthshaking traffic and the grim, unspeakable looks zooming past behind glass. He had to quit! Whatever it was he was doing. Oh yes, hitching—he lowered his arm. But after that, his head trip kept rushing and swerving among blurry inner goings-on, much like the traffic. It was getting easy to mix up the two, in fact. Then, out of nowhere, presumably his skull, said a traffic cop: "However strong and strange your mental pictures get, don't forget where you are and wander onto the road." Later, urgently: "Get away from the freeway—*without stepping into traffic!*"

Then there came into his mind's eye a busy, shaded street above the ramp. He'd have to cross that again to get away! He knew his timing would be off for the job. (There came a fleeting, tactile feeling in his bones of death on impact by steel and hard rubber.) Later, if he got by *those* fast lanes of asphalt, he might yet get all confused in their environing megalopolis, stray into a neighborhood without traffic lights, get run over elsewhere. His everyday uneasiness nigh barreling cars and trucks exaggerated into distress. And to make matters worse, all the motorists hurrying on seemed to stare at him so harshly that he had trouble making up his mind. *"Uh, oh! What should I do? What should I do here and now?"*

With too many loud machines about, green plants stand for safety, he reasoned, barring chainsaws. A few paces behind him, he crawled under a dusty, obscure bush. One planted to decorate California interstates. Stashed his carcass there to sit out his temporary mindset and then stayed put, still as a mouse, without taking in how many hours were going by. Where all he could see was a bunch of twigs and sparse leaves in dark silhouette against scraps of glaring pavement. Meanwhile, the concrete strip persisted with all its noisy, stinking nearness—a few yards away, sudden death on the fly! SWOOSH! SWOOSH! BARRROOM!

While going on all fours through a hole in the shrubbery before settling down, there came an image: "I'm a mouse!" An image that summed up his feelings and put him on the scent of his subsequent leading insight. Although it derived from an oversight, really: getting too high. Making him now look down on Zeke, small as a mouse, under the bush, from way up. To where it flared up at him that the worst fate was to be overanxious and gentle, yet have the person of a male. (WWRRROGGG! A nerve-shattering motorcycle roared by, and he flinched.) His reflexes to the likes of that were often in contradiction to his looked-for role.

It only got worse the deeper he delved, behind his symmetrical, nice-looking features. Nosing about internally, he sniffed out the stubborn remnants of recent slights, snubs, and affronts, along with some fossil recollections of kicks in the pants. There came reflections on his mousey body language, too. Seeing how routinely he scratched his scalp or pawed his ears. All of it serving to pinpoint a painful realization, which he knew all too well. That he was less aggressive than most guys, slower to anger and low in the pecking order. A mouse!

Then the hashish brought up and ran some well-worn case history from his teens, yet serviceable for self-loathing.

Prelude

Already, he was into his twenties, with no change in sight! He was hurting for something more upbeat after that. Certainly, he *had* been more afraid of fighting than most boys back on his stamping ground. Yet, more than most, he was well-equipped with empathy ("women's intuition"). Which included being observant of other's reactions to him. Reassuring, since, among other things, this gave warning of their potential for violence.

With a mousey giggle, he dove down a new conceptual tunnel to depict the violent as rats. How it was—mouse number one amidst vicious, heavyset rats. Ordinarily, though, he could make out a rat plainer in the dim light of first encounter than it could see what he was. So, in practice, he wasn't such easy prey. What with that advantage and his teens gone, he now bore less hostility toward rats—or that's what he liked to believe of late.

Could be he was only coming down, but gradually, as he pondered the other lab animals scampering about, he came to be aware of a third kind: guinea pigs. Critters tougher than mice, yet not prone to malevolence like rats. Over the years, many of his school chums had been guinea pigs.

> *"We who thirst for reason want to look our experiences as straight in the eye as if they represented a scientific experiment. We ourselves want to be our experiments and guinea pigs."*
> —Friedrich Nietzsche

Right. What about all the guinea pigs he'd met? More majestic than mice, more dependable than rats, his old allies they were. Since both mice and guinea pigs differed from rats in sharing one significant inclination: neither condoned brute force. Only rats threatened or went in for it much. The other two species of rodent did not—emergencies excepted.

Guinea pigs were unlike mice in one important way. That they were lusty enough to have recourse to violence or, at any rate, threaten it passably well as a deterrent. Mice, adversely affected by traumas or their genes, cowards down to their toes, presumed themselves helpless in dealing with rats or other hazards, and so often were.

At this stage in his seminal imaginings, for the animal act before Zeke's eyes to keep his rapt attention, it needed some sex, too. So there it was. Zeke couldn't help noticing that the majority of females are mice, though there be a sizable minority of guinea pigs among them, and even a sprinkling of rats. Nor, chewing over the nature of things, could he shrink from the conclusion that the majority of males are guinea pigs, though with sizable minorities of both mice and rats. The ratios seemed about, for males, 1 mouse : 4 guinea pigs : 1 rat. For females, 3.9 mice : 2 guinea pigs : .1 rat. (Note: this statistical typology may only apply to their public deportment; with some female guinea pigs throwing frying pans and so forth on their home territory, and she-mice bolder there, too.)

All breeds of varmint dressed and acted out of character now and then, so a hasty estimate was tricky. For instance, while dumber rats were often, though not all, noisy and obnoxious—charged with strident, loutish self-assurance—sophisticated ones could fulfill a more restrained leading role. They might have down civility with smiles attached. Many rats could easily be taken, at first, for guinea pigs—or vice versa. But, with those male mice who were not thoroughly

Prelude

effeminate and smiley for the duration, it was another story. Mostly they looked worried. And if courteous, that was due as much to persistent uneasiness about rats as to conscientiousness. Their good behavior seemed less voluntary, more automatic. As for female mice, they smiled a great deal—except the moody ones.

Juvenile Zeke yearned to be a guinea pig, but was a mouse. There, under any adjustable aspects of his personality was a fairly stable quality of mind. Female mice yearned to be guinea pigs, too, many of them, on the testimony of the media—thoroughly modern, empowered somebodies with higher salaries. Likewise, older and wiser rats chose to be seen as guinea pigs much of the time. Inasmuch as making noises like a guinea pig enabled some to get away with more cheese and mate with more females without needlessly alarming their victims, customers, or coworkers. (Another layer of complexity came from aging. Some of the mice hardened as middle age got to them; some of the rats softened.)

Mutual cooperation was largely to all three species' advantage. What a turmoil of gentleness, civility, and muscle-flexing ensued as three breeds of rodent experimented with integration. Many lab critters who weren't guinea pig through and through strove to persuade themselves, or anyone keeping an eye on them, of their guinea-pigness. All the while, the indisputable guinea pigs, along with aspiring pretenders, tried encouraging mice to be more like themselves—bringing to bear a variety of rewards and punishments, ranging from admiration and wealth to gossip and psychotherapy. While flagrant male mice and nefarious rats were crushed

Prelude

with ridicule, prison, and so forth. Yet, plausibly virtuous, tax-paying rodents were mostly judged guinea pigs, given the benefit of the doubt. (Incidentally, it is a criminal misconception, while doing time at the zoo, that all snitches are "rats." When they also may in fact be convicted guinea pigs or mice.)

Using for symbolic characterization three lab animals did fine for making categories of disposition memorable, he thought. But why select fierceness, or its absence, as their defining attribute? Why? Because a rodent's attitude regarding killer instinct, and exercise thereof, not their other traits or opinions or capacities, is the aspect of psyche and conduct most productive for sorting them out. The foremost concern of moral codes and laws, after all, as for the mouse on the street, is in preservation of life and limb. Bloody bad is worse than other kinds of bad.

Making use of multiple moral criteria, as with "the righteous vs. sinners" or "the decent vs. indecent" is too broad and indefinite to do the job. Such frames of reference de-emphasize ferocity in bundling it with less-telling characteristics. They clutter the gravest moral concern. In Zeke's experience, there were unrighteous and indecently sneaky mice and corrupt guinea pigs out there with all those brutal rats (who might even, on the side, do some noble deeds, too).

The majority of mature rodents, once their near-universal taste for cheese is gratified, take parts in acting respectable; the styles of their theatrics, nonetheless, vary widely. And the major variable among them, so far as Zeke could see, centered on rat faith in the respectability of ferocity. In the drama of

Prelude

day-to-day existence, how blatantly feisty should a rodent hold forth? How laudable is violence as a highlight of their behavioral pattern? Propriety had never quite prevailed in making violent displays obsolete. Thus, with Christianity in decline, Zeke was keeping body and soul together in a disorderly lab, where rat notions of appropriate behavior clashed with guinea pig principles and laws on the issue. As a mouse, though, and lacking forcefulness in his support of nonviolence, he was not getting much respect from either camp.

Not getting much sex, either. Near all female guinea pigs and most female mice were drawn to male guinea pigs. Those stately go-getters whose poise, bulk, likely salaries, and the rest signaled fitness. While, seemingly unbeknownst to the euphemistically inclined, they also relied upon coming home to a talent for defensive threat in a mate. Defensive only—not offensive. Size and a manly mug should do it. Unfortunately, many were tardy at working things out after getting saddled with an offensive rat in lieu of a tolerable guinea pig.

Yet, although Zeke had no use for them, rats were widely seen as good enough for sex. Of which ritual, frolicsome intimidation and appeasement are principal ingredients. Most guinea pigs did okay, too. So relatively few female rodents ever got around to sampling those sensational male mice—massage their specialty. It was either that, or they'd all take off.

Beneath his burning bush, it all came together. That arcane borderland by a California freeway of smog, heat, and roar finally conveyed how it is. At the rising of a semi-transparent smog curtain, as upon a nickelodeon screen in murky, yellowish light,

Prelude

Zeke saw what was going on through the foliage. Trapped in an animated cartoon! It all flashed and snarled by his shadowy front-row seat: thundering herds of impalas, mustangs with legs of steel, tiger-tanked falcons and hawks, firebirds, bullydog trucks, wildcats, and there went Wile E. Coyote in person. But, essentially, it was a dehumanizing rat race.

Ratmobiles driving the cloverleaves of a maze, or undergoing the operant conditioning of traffic signs and lights. The positive reinforcement of compliantly going along in line, every bit like an adult motorist, rewarded many. The negative ones of traffic jams, cops, breakdowns, and accidents punished others. And, oh wow, some rodents cruised by in luxury vehicles—conspicuous rewards for rat-racing prowess. Objectively, the freeway was a behaviorist maze; subjectively, that afternoon, poor little Zeke trembled at becoming road kill.

Wait! His new awareness of his fellow creatures on Gaia almost had the makings of a New Age theology or, leastways, a new totemic mythology. Its spotty dogma a synthesis of behaviorist and Disney perspectives on rodents. All of them under perpetual observation by a celestial Lab Technician? Notwithstanding, despite his Mouseketeer faith in the Magic Kingdom up ahead, Zeke fretted that his roadside realm of rising smog was too secular. Didn't these heavy masses of hurtling substance before his red eyes seem somehow unspiritual, too worldly? Leave the whole mess for science, then: a new taxonomy for personality psychology! A pioneering trait hypothesis if ever he knew what was what. *Eurekallua!*

Afterwards, Zeke realized its further utility. That, beyond mere theory, it was a workaday tool! Wielding it could add to

Prelude

his safety and comfort. Throw another thick analogue upon the fires of illumination to keep off the rats. Becoming wise to them as an indigenous subspecies, their breathing, lurking presence would be easier to detect. As comparatively few rats were smooth enough to consistently hide their liking for brutality. On the contrary, many made boast of it, swaggered, and challenged. Or, to bare their fang,s they smirked, sniggered, or stared, mostly, but now and again taunted.

Mouse acquaintanceship protocol #1: Avoid the company of explicit rats. Mouse acquaintanceship protocol #2: Choose the company of other mice or guinea pigs, else remain aloof.

Mice, in review, are those little guys, both genders, more afraid of injury to their corporeal parts and also more susceptible to emotional scarring. Who are thus disturbed by the presence of rats, real or imagined. Yet, on the bright side, more than rats, they know about what's going through both their own and others' noodles—of depths below the sociable surface. Which is why Zeke, in all his days of bumming, never met a very empathetic or introspective rat. They were shallower that way. (Even though their estuary might be in flood with some political or religious belief, awash in their mouth like a stray crab.)

Early in his travels, when Zeke reached northern California, he lapsed into a recurring pattern of reverie. First off, there was clear remembrance, before leaving home, of his having thoughts about being in a way-off region on the map: northern California. Now, dreamlike, in looking around, he was actually *there*. "I'm in California!" It was pretty as a picture! As if the

Prelude

map diagram of California had transformed into woods and fields. "I'm here!" In a topography with as much presence as New England, but of another sort.

Walking through sunshiny Sonoma countryside, he was visualizing expansive white bubbles of joy rising up and bursting in his chest. Being there among the new smells of eucalyptus, live oak, and fennel. How far he was! Echoes of a childhood trip to a magic park hid in his all-grown-up-now dream of distance. Was this the appeal of traveling in its essence? But all of this came during breaks from his first stint in the city.

He strolled Haight Street. The air held whiffs of incense, and the sidewalks set forth eccentricity, both sexes with long hair and strange "threads." A far-out, deviant medley of tie-dyes and colored prints, along with eclectic period and ethnic outfits. All day and evening, casual costume processions, mixing with the mundane. Many way out, but for such standard details—something else again—as long hair and beards, sandals or bare feet, and patchouli perfume. Which longer-lasting customs of grooming gave the mushrooming subculture an aura of being no mere sometime thing. It gave a more unified aspect to its otherwise wayward grooviness. They impressed as being less cowed by convention than like drably dressed short-hairs in other neighborhoods.

Zeke had been eager to come and go among hippies. Driven by their curious publicity, for they filled his media exposure. The Haight-Ashbury district in San Francisco was said to be their home. "Where it's all happening!" it was broadcast. So there he was, late in the 1967 Summer

Prelude

of Love. There amongst the exuberant "good vibes" on its streets. Where in the air rattled a new slang, used with more frequency than obscenities. How the hairy "hip" established themselves "in."

Hip-hurray! There was cheerful expectation in the air, too. As if a singular "head trip" on psychedelics had sprouted wings and fluttered throughout collective awareness as an inescapable new force of fashion. A utopian vision spontaneously come true. The anarchistic millennium automatically, willy-nilly, manifesting.

Soon after arrival, Zeke was seeking peace of mind in the Golden Gate Park Panhandle near Oak and Masonic. For his regular self-critical musings were exacerbated by city rumble and the crowd. Although a few strangers on the street had smiled, thereabouts, within a peculiarly "laid-back" and cooperative urban district.

At precisely that crucial juncture, he took the plunge and spoke to somebody. Daring to pass himself off as a more extroverted hick than he was for real, he asked a "head" groomed only moderately hip: "Which way to the love?" Whereupon, in place of well-deserved mockery for that ice-breaker, he was shown to a "crash pad," which filled with crashers as the evening drifted by. There Zeke got acquainted with John, another newcomer close to his own age. A tall, heavyset cowboy, with whom Zeke strung along next day. For his new partner knew where there was "grass." (As every cowboy and cowgirl should.) It would be at a party to which he'd been invited.

Neither of them had ever tried it. Being a mouse, Zeke was hesitant at first, but then made up his mind to do as the

Prelude

hippies and big strong cowboys did—chance it. At a Fell St. house fronting on the panhandle, a lovely midtown setting; one among many Victorians with bay windows, two- or three-story "carpenters' gothic" fretwork on their wooden façades, and painted in pastel tints.

They shared a "joint." After only a few "tokes," the ranch hand began laughing uproariously. Then he couldn't quit. "HA! HA! HA! HA! HA! HA! HA! HA! HA! HA! HA! . . ." On and on. Those who lived there were getting really worried, after he went on so long. Two guys lugged him into the next room to lie down on a bed. He was barely catching his breath. They tried to calm and quiet him—shaking or pleading with him—but he was beyond self-control, as if incessantly coughing from a sore throat, totally "freaked out." He was having way too much fun!

In the living room again, from John's bedside, stifled by the kooky ambiance, Zeke only felt "normal." "How do you feel?" someone who seemed to be far-off asked him, and that's what he seemed to say. Regard for what words were gliding from his mouth was a little slack, was all. Real hippies weren't supposed to be normal. But his cowboy companion had him uneasy about letting go. Then another remote message came in. This time, in a relaxed feminine voice, describing what sensation in herself she noticed. "And you might, too." Then gradually, after a couple more puffs, he did notice it.

In response, he lay down for hours, his back on the carpet, letting his thoughts wander, or taking a good look at a few water stains on the ceiling. (The better you feel, the less time matters.) But he was too close to the front door, where some new arrivals later on greeted whoever were his host and hostess. One fellow asked, "What's the function of that?" standing above him and pointing.

Zeke thought him very witty. As it happened, he was feeling about like an inanimate object at that stage—absolutely incapable of budging. Did he function mainly as a laugh-starting device? He broke out laughing. Then, so did some of those above. And the next thing Zeke perceived was that he'd quit laughing. So reassuring, his continuing ability to manage his emotions.

Abruptly, the cowboy who brought him went silent. As the host or somebody assisted him a few blocks to the fabulous Free Clinic. Zeke didn't see him again. He might have died laughing for all he knew or heard, having lost track of all "rapping" and other goings-on in the room, having gone into himself and closed the door behind him. From whence, after a while, he concluded that marijuana was head and shoulders above alcohol for the introspective, such as he, but was not for everybody.

Zeke got to be desk clerk in a cheap hotel south of Market St. Where, only a few months of soaking up the local ethos, and his rising consciousness knew the tremor of living in The Most Consequential Era in the History of Humanity. Agitation about The People and peace prevailed. The times, they were a changin'. Their *movement* would soon build a better world, starting with California. Magic, mystery, nonconformity, authenticity, spontaneity: all spreading like weed! Competition, greed, mistrust: all dying out. Flower power!

On a different yet equally liberated level of rising consciousness was progressive politics. Christianity might be on the skids, but moral education marched on, at least for a little ways. *Clomp! Clomp! Clomp!* Progress on parade. Ethically uplifting slogans and sentiments were there for the shouting. One hot movement came on the heels of another. None of them linked with stuff going on for a while—always about brand-new *issues*. Journalism, the fast-food of history.

Capitalism was evil, of course, but would soon be overthrown by the will of the people. For as the impression of God's will faded, that of man's (and woman's) will gained weight. Humanity would prevail on its own! Through more education, and thanks to those well-intentioned science-loving folks squatting behind mass communications. Men *and* women would set the world aright (aleft). For science was seen as the cause of historical change more than as its effect. Or more than science's causes and effects were seen both together as an inevitable process.

At any rate, it flattered *his generation* to believe they lived in uniquely revolutionary times. And it flattered Zeke, in particular, to fantasize he was seated in the cockpit of the great American politico-scientific spacecraft flying upward and onward in the direction of world unity and liberated lives. Anti-technologists were taking control of the ship. Right there in the Bay Area, they were, where he wasn't missing out on any of the modernity.

While high out there, unfortunately, the six o'clock news off-and-on impressed upon him that he was sitting too near the forefront of the accelerating ship for comfort. It was all

Prelude

coming true, like heads in the park were saying—a crash any day now! The nation in crisis, like a meteor field, with the dangers of bloody revolution, anarchy, and their fascist repression like slobbering space-monsters lying in wait beyond. Sinister events and portents were everywhere!

Then a minor earthquake struck while he was sitting on the toilet in a claustrophobic men's room. But where was he? Downtown San Francisco! What if the whole thing collapsed and buried him just like that forever? Yup, in that town his seat of consciousness could rise only so far, hinged to the bowl as it was, and given the ominous insecurity of his situation. "San Francisco": he'd seen the movie!

Zeke liked the metro nether world when it was foggy, and nothing shaking. Murky, chilly weather out the window made his ratty hotel rooms seem like the order of the day. It made his regret over wasting outdoor sunlight recede. Besides which, his room gave him immunity from the eyes of others. Yet, even on the street during necessary errands, some days were coolish enough to cover up his stringiness with a sweater, swing along, and not be singled out by strangers.

Only rarely was he able to look objectively into the mirror. Pride generally kept him from seeing what was there. His androgynous visage: wide-eyed, rosy-cheeked, with long eyelashes, pale skin, and rococo hair. His body, in those days, was stooped and puny. He looked like a wilting houseplant with middle- to upper-class roots that hadn't been properly watered. He toyed with the thought that his glands were defective.

Prelude

More than once, with the Beetles and a caste of thousands as model, he hankered after longer hair. But with his giraffe's neck and waves, each time, he began losing his nerve about when it attained his ear lobes. And his beard—red, thin, and scratchy—was not much comfort, either. Undeniably, his auburn hair was too bushy and pretty to be *with-it*, he was eventually driven to admit. Although, for a time, it made buying dope easier.

His looks contributed to his embarrassment, as did his rut of walking about within cities. Although amateurish self-analysis from a few self-help publications seemed to indicate that he was suffering from over-socialization (not overpopulation). Indicated that, unless he could retain the conviction that he, yours truly, was Jesus Christ, all-knowing and good, he would feel among others minutely scrutinized and judged wanting. (And this intellectual breakthrough was kept in a separate compartment of mind from the particulars of his physique.)

As well they might, girls and employers were fleeing him on sight, but other strangers hung around to stomp his self-assurance, or what there was of it. There were occasional whistles or jeers on the street, and not only from blacks. Some of the whistles were probably misdirected come-on's from gay rats, though more were from straight rats hassling a presumed gay. A table of white beer drinkers once hee-hawed at him for being "lonely" when he asked for a hotdog in a bar.

Would-be longhaired insiders, both genders, pronounced their "Oh wow!"-s upon him for the way he looked—not our

Prelude

sort, not totally hip. (The commonplace "Wow" was "Mom" lying on her back, and expressed a position of settled passive prerogative.) From midlife men in suits or otherwise came troubled looks out of nowhere that said, "Why didn't his generation mature?" (Or some might be wondering why such a nice-looking boy had turned gay, although in those days homosexuality wasn't publicized much.)

San Francisco was such a sightly city, but many of its neighborhoods held petty tormentors, were bug-infested. In spite of which, some of the put-downs coming his way, in review, seemed only inventions of his own edgy mind. Which suggested the mental-health insight that looking more like a mouse than like a rat was as sure a way for a dude to ripen a neurosis in the city as going without this or that vitamin was of catching a cold.

Even Haight Street was coming down with a contagious chill. There were more rats about. "Paranoia" was the up-and-coming buzzword. Because guys with less-sensitive antennae than your average male mouse more often didn't know whom they could trust. So that, after the first groovy few years, all were breaking out in identical blue denim shirts to match their jeans—hiding themselves. Then, after the tourist buses came speed freaks, wearing motorcycles and no-nonsense black leather jackets. Love beads and the blanket people were near extinction. What a thing!

Other parts of the city that he zipped through now and then were looking unhealthy, too. For example, he felt embarrassed slouching through white-bread shopping districts midtown

Prelude

or malls in the suburbs. Sickening luxury, and he might be mistaken for a denizen, him with his pink-and-vanilla winter complexion. Out of his preferred habitat there, he was. Apt to be found wanting in his supporting role as hip urbanite, Zeke began to loathe some parts of his San Francisco stage set, as if they were parts of *him*. Such as Nob Hill, where he could fancy his critics were harsher and ever so many.

But *he* was also an amateur drama critic! And he was picking up on overtones of stage fright emanating from wealth. Yes, any tenseness or diffidence that he spied in persons dressed for success was understandable. As nice-looking garments, fine skin, and other valuable personal effects were looking hideously bourgeois, middlebrow, and unfashionable. What's more, he was sensing disapproval of his very own skin—with him in it—from blacks, along with his getup and haircut from most whites. If everybody had *their* way, they'd give him such a makeover! More than likely, though, he was projecting most all the censure in the air out of his own anxieties about who he was and how he looked. Smack onto innocent passersby, fallout from his wishy-washy identity.

However that may be, after lousy taste in sportswear, and dressing up in formal business attire, what looked most awkward was dressing middle-class semi-hip. *His* look! So that Zeke was inclined to think that something—the radicals in Berkeley? the Martians? TV? grass?—was making one and all hypersensitive to social inequality. *Wait!* Hypersensitive to social *variety*—was that it? Were the insidious mass media flooding culture with a bigger selection of exemplary comparison models—vicarious acquaintances—and thereby raising its audience's rate of self-doubt or, in the ambitious, envy?

In Zeke's case, and in California, whatever was responsible, it would have him ashamed that his life was too easy, privileged, and secure. (Despite his de facto poverty and insecurity.) Those secret vibes of radical righteousness made him out to be no less than a guilty citizen of an overdeveloped country, which he wasn't doing enough to oppose or take over or whatnot. So much so that he could almost feel on the verge of turning heroic class struggler, ready to strike blows against the empire—*but* he just wasn't right for the part.

Then, there was the ongoing Vietnam War, too, as another possibility for penance. Although not as alluring a movement as those for human potential or sexual freedom or psychedelic drugs, he certainly wasn't opposed to peace. And so Zeke got caught up in a couple mass demonstrations, buried in the midst of smiling crowds. Magnetically irresistible, they were. With smiles all round, confidently striking massive blows for nonviolence! Ordinarily, he disliked crowds, though.

Our nature boy was picturing to his humble self an abode far off the streetcar track, well away from San Francisco. Ultimately, he got around to it. With his hair no longer than it had to be, but still in his bell-bottomed jeans, he sequestered in Marin County. Where, for long, he lingered in a lean-to in a well-hidden spot on the lower slopes of Mt. Tamalpais, not so far from Stinson Beach.

Jazzing up the hushed redwood spell of that peninsula was some of the most raucous nightlife ever attended. No end

Prelude

of field mice, there were, with inexhaustible owls, with other strange-sounding night birds, and with coyote howls. Then, all day: quail, buzzards, hawks. While many little brown, black, and gray feathered friends chirped and did their bit, too, along with the smallest deer he'd seen. Once, soon after dawn, he took in a family of bobcats frolicking on a log.

He only thumbed his way into the city for supplies and to sell plasma at the blood bank. On the two-laner into the freeway, he went, looking out over a blue-black, white-speckled sea. Then, it was over the Golden Gate bridge. Whereupon, the city was every time, reassuringly, there where he left it. Now and again, though, the Bird-and-mouseman of Marin flitted upstate, into the Pacific Northwest. As in those heady days, hitchhiking in North America was easy.

Hitching ease may be a good indication of how much trust, cooperation, and helpfulness is left in a modern nation—among country dwellers and bohemians, at any rate. Good for doing informal spot-checks, it is. Although, in modern, car-saturated societies, hitchhiking is apt to furnish a better sample of that than in developing countries. Since, where cars are less common, such data may be compromised by upper-class noblesse oblige, or the sheer novelty value of obvious outsiders.

Anyway, getting a lift on the West Coast right then was simple enough, but getting in on a collective farm was hairy. Zeke was denied entry or continuing residence quite a few times after making bold to ask plausibly hip guinea pigs to stay over. In the end, the two or three who apparently had the say, on each farm, always turned him out or away. Although always while pretending it was out of their hands—authority

Prelude

being a no-no. A couple of the smoother, though, at his send-off, presented him with the tactful pretext that he looked like a nark. (Virile and longhaired!) When not among totally paranoid pot farmers, though, realer reasons were more like his not smiling enough and hair too short. As mostly they were after ever-grinning extroverts with acceptable hairdos, much like his alma mater—beneath their tresses, they were fraternity boys yammering away. A "nark": at least they weren't calling him a "dork" anymore. Moreover, an unfavorable boy/girl ratio out of town counted heavily against him, too. And so his career path as a hippie hit a plateau.

Back to the hideout: to his mountainside shelter on Mt. Tam. Where he gave some thought to the counterculture. Which he only rounded out years later.

It seems as though various historians have remarked that one of the longer-range ill effects of war is upon civilian morals and manners. Primarily afterwards, when the soldiers come home. But perhaps an ongoing overseas war may also have a *positive* effect upon morals and behavior on the home front—at least temporarily. For one minor thing, most notably among civilian males, the Vietnam war might be said to have increased freedom of self-expression in grooming.

Certainly in the American '60s and '70s it did. When so many rats and hardened guinea pigs were in the military overseas. Most fighting obediently for their country, teamwork, their draft board, or their pay, but a few from craving explosions, bloodshed, and other exciting disasters; whether or not they'd admit it. Nonetheless, from whatever mixture of motive, aggressive boys—those more likely to bully and fight—were more often out of the picture in those days, so culture and personal style back home turned more girlish.

Young men with long hair flaunting everywhere, longer and longer. No longer so afraid to hint they had sensitivity and vulnerability. While "rap-" or "head trip"-inducing psychedelic drugs, when not occasions of mystical experience, mostly kept their smiles in place, anyhow. Making them look and feel more human, which is to say more ethical, which is to imply more female. Inasmuch as girls typically have finer morals than boys.

The ethos lay feminizing, amid its peace signs, for two decades or so. While countercultural celebrations and "families," big and small, attempted to encourage and preserve the utopian communal ideal of love and togetherness. While marches and movements provided yet more solidarity and handholding for many—girls and civilian boys. The conscientious protested the war. Then it ended, most of the bad boys came home, and down came all kinds of moral decay like: speedy or mind-numbing addictive drugs, gang activity, mass shootings, short hair, tattoos to hide needle tracks, and black shirts. Black being the color of authority and formality (or crime, or fat). The moral pendulum, in swinging back, overcompensated for the multicolor days of flower-power.

The Vietnam War ended April 30, 1975. A pertinent statistic: the number of mass shootings from 1949 through 1975 with 10 or more fatalities was 3. The number of mass shootings from 1976 through 2018 with 10 or more fatalities was 22. The second period is 1.62 times longer, but within it the number of mass shootings with 10 or more fatalities is

7.33 times larger! Not that veterans were directly to blame for most of the increase. It was more like the entire post-Vietnam era took a downturn and them with it.

Of course, civilization back home may not receive the same temporary boost during the course of all or even most wars. For that to occur, broadcast media may have to be not only pervasive but also mostly free in their programming. Enough to pass along the symbols, catchphrases, and pictures of a new youth counterculture emerging. While a wartime economy makes jobs easy to come by. Yet, if these and maybe other things align just so among the planets again—unrestricted media, a high employment rate, legal grass, and a big overseas war—there may dawn another 20 years or so of Aquarius.

Now, how do civilian gun massacres come into fashion? Among other important factors, they depend upon the broadcast media again, plus internet, to some extent. Insofar as these play to the fantasies of a much smaller, crazier set of trendy people than hippies. Homicidal maniacs, going by their live interviews and biographies on TV, by and large, are responding to deep-seated impulses to kill, of which they may or may not be aware. Thus, they may be psychopathic, with an ambition for fame, and like guns, but even so may need assistance in thinking up just what to make of their lives—exactly when and how to act out their compulsions.

The media help them visualize that—how to fully express themselves. Cable television instructs and releases them with daily programming devoted to the careers of violent criminals, even granting some of these the status of "famous" or "legendary."

Serial or mass killers may bring higher ratings, but some shows are, pure and simple, devoted to "copycat killers" of however many. Proving station employees aren't entirely ignorant of their own bloody role. Supplying nutcases with comrade-in-arms imitation models of unconventional behavior. Then we have terrorist recruitment over the internet, too, for the ideologically challenged. Plus, mass-shooting videos are online.

In Zeke's hippie heydays, hitting the trail was getting away from it all. "All" encompassed most everyone that he had to either talk or listen to at length, and cities. All that gone, and there he was, encircled by wide-open spaces or woods. Where a reliably cheerful humor would come over him as he meandered through fine samples of the outdoors unaccompanied. Typically it replenished him within an hour of entering such an ambience. And so, with more care than for his address booklet, Zeke kept lists of beauty spots. Solitude got to be his dominant want.

In some locations, out in the open air, the ease from enchanting scenery in other-worldly quiet informed him of his soul's priority. More by receiving an impression than understanding it. Heartland. Only later did Zeke get a slippery grip on a concept of the beautiful. So that he could come to terms with what qualities his "beauty spots" had in common.

Right off, though, Zeke perceived that regions of miraculous charm should be sensed up close and slow-paced. Which was why, by his lights, the prime methods of motion through them should only be walking, swimming, and small-boating. Anything else ridden, such as a bicycle or horse, would tend to be too swift or elevated, and would limit access. (Not counting bikes ridden to trailheads.)

Thus, in going on a journey, from fairly early, Zeke's foremost goals became either trails or primo snorkeling beaches. Cities soon shed their glamour. And, contrary to what they say about costly cruises, getting there (arriving at his out-of-town destinations) was more fun than getting *to* them. Which was about a third of the fun, tops. (Along with ¾ of the bother.) Nevertheless, a solid estimate of the fun genuinely up for grabs in some section of the boonies could seldom be made before getting there and stepping out.

His three focal types of transport for passing through selected lands and sea yielded fringe benefits—physical exercise, for one. But also, according to a lagging authority on the subject: slow-going, muscular modes of locomotion are more effective cures for minor depression, scourge of civilization, than any other non-drug therapy now available. What's more, going off into naturalness, Zeke learned on his own, also relieves anxiety fast, fast, fast! (Other than in house mice it did. Zeke was a field mouse.) Hence, walking became an inviting pastime for an immature introvert, waiting to get over an annoying phase, keeping in shape for better days ahead. Nature, refuge of misfits.

A stronger motivation for continuing to hike or swim in his later adulthood became less noticeably the leaving behind of humankind and more a desire for natural beauty and quiet. These made wilderness or coral shores rewarding. Almost invariably, they put him in a good mood. Even where people or other bits of civilization were scattered along a trail or beach, their interruptions became no worse than brief static while listening to radio music. But there was another incentive for going out and about, too. The loveliness of nature often generated creative thought: its next-best payoff. When, similarly, a trickle of other walkers or vehicles through someplace did not automatically switch off stimulating brainwaves. Now and then, their occurrence instead energized musings.

So here the beaten path reverts to people and all. To everybody met everywhere on the road, severally and as a whole. Well, mostly, Zeke had a hunch that out-and-out withdrawal onto roundabout ways gave his active fancy more of the exercise it wanted than hanging about a city street, whether domestic or foreign. That flights of fancy went farther out of town. At times, though, he wasn't so sure. In town, striking the flint or steel of alien intelligence could also give a light, as sparks of impression flew.

Both means to an end are promising, depending upon mood, age, and temperament. And also depending upon the caliber of strangeness in strangers. Though rare they might be, he'd come across some amazing specimens like Gabriel, especially when younger—brazen materialists and whatnot.

There was a militant named or renamed Gabriel whom he met in San Francisco once. Where he made himself sound like a low-key public figure of his day ('70s.). Seeing as how nights he regularly crashed in the homes of various friends, or that was his first story. A hunky extrovert, he blew his own horn—literally—on a back street sidewalk: jazz trumpet. Licks, mostly, not entire pieces. Sometimes he'd put down his case

Prelude

for contributions and sometimes not. Either way, a difficult man to ignore. For his speech, too, was compelling, between musical interludes. He could discourse on several topics with extraordinary logic, speed, and precision. What was amiss with capitalism was his preferred rap, however.

Both his free music-making and then his rhetoric caught Zeke's ear. Who at first was almost overwhelmed with brain envy. Subsequently, though, this archangel of Marxism, queried about his gift of gab, admitted having a photographic memory. With language he improvised less; often reciting riffs he'd read or authored. Howsoever, his was a prodigious talent for lecturing. Out poured tortuous analyses of economics and politics, with illustrations from the record of the past. Zeke, our college dropout, had never gotten so close to an ideologue before.

"Who would I be quoting today if I quoted you?" was one among many things that Zeke, after the fact, saw that he should have said. For Zeke's special flair was in hitting upon clever phrases that he should have come up with in former discussions, dreaming up rather than remembering. Or had he actually said almost that? His retention of speech, even his own, was mediocre. Same as with big ideas absorbed, he couldn't do more off the top of his head than paraphrase. Anyway, they once said something to the effect:

Zeke: "Didn't Marx say that socialist revolution was inevitable?"

Gabe: "Yes!"

Zeke: "Then why bother to proselytize? Why not devote yourself to blowing trumpet?"

Prelude

Gabe: "Da. Da. Daa. Da. Daa. Da Da. Da Daa. Da. Daaah!"

Zeke was fascinated by Gabe's total recall and began seeing him almost daily. Gabe once muttered that people were apt to think them gay. Zeke said that he was not, though he attracted his share, taking Gabe's comment as a careless jibe from a bad mood. But, he later conjectured, his reply to it only raised Gabe's suspicion in another quarter.

After a few days, Gabe confessed to having a permanent abode and led the way to an inexpensive furnished room. In going, though, they seemed to be pursuing an indirect course up and down parallel streets and off through a couple alleys. Whereupon, Zeke asked Gabe jokingly if he worried someone might follow them. His reply was a tight smile.

When they got there, though, Gabe *did* comment upon how painstaking he'd been in hunting down habitation that the cops or secret service couldn't trace. "Secret Service?" While thinking that over, Zeke took in the room. It, too, was far from expected. Jokingly, again, Zeke expressed concern that his landlord might inform on him when he saw how he'd remodeled. For the furniture was all stacked against one wall, apart from one mattress on the floor, and another wedged up against the wall behind it. Gabe didn't laugh at the thought his landlord might be an informer, as Zeke wanted, but his sense of humor wasn't much.

"Yoga is the reason for the arrangement," he said. "The aftereffect of a drug they gave me in prison was spinal pain. I treat it by standing on my head awhile daily. More blood to my brain boosts concentration, too. My brain needs blood—another thing I learned in prison." He stepped onto the floor mattress and urged Zeke to do the same. Who did, anticipating a yoga demonstration.

Then, after a short while, in which nothing memorable was said, the subject being landlords, Gabe suddenly snarled, "Who are you? Who sent you?" Had Zeke misspoken? He didn't see how. Then it happened very quickly: Gabe twisted his shirt into a tight, solid grip and pressed the blade of a knife from somewhere against his throat. Then he turned and nudged him back against the wall mattress.

Through Zeke flashed the fervent hope that Gabe's interrogation was such a trite piece of movie crazy-talk that he wasn't serious. Only a ratty practical joke, no more—to be rid of him fast after having lost patience with the rate of his conversion. Quite a few heavy heartbeats after, though, no grin had peeped out. Gabe only repeated himself louder, far from smiling.

Zeke's inner police detective at that point said "Tell the truth." Fortunately, he was unemployed; no one sent him anywhere. And further, truth was, his lively interest in Gabe came from an unsuspected liking for arguing politics with one of his intelligence. With wide-eyed innocence, Zeke denied any connection with the police or other government agencies. "Do I look like a cop?" There he may have gone too far. (Attempting to lull him with more stale dialogue.) But after what seemed a very long pause, Gabe withdrew the knife. Only to roughly shake him. "Are you queer?" Zeke denied that one, too. "I told you before."

Prelude

Gabe let go. Zeke made soothing intonations about friendship and respect; for good measure, he brought in his esteem for Marx. Was it the width of his eyes or, to a musician's ear, his sincere vocal style that saved him? Assuredly it wasn't karate or a concealed weapon, as in action flicks. No, even a knife-wielding, paranoid fanatic must have known damn well that few genuine secret agents could portray so persuasively fright and sincerity.

In a pinch, despite a lackluster personality, Zeke had salvaged and reshaped the emotional charge from terror to lend his tone of speech authenticity. Also, simply looking harmless—at which he was good—may buy time. All during the business, Zeke was on guard not to look or sound, much less behave, like a worthy foe. Unless cut.

Gabe calmed down and warily pocketed his knife. Any scheme he may have momentarily or longer entertained about doing a murder for the Party was probably gone. His impulsiveness spent, or his bonkers plan fully accomplished, or so Zeke hoped as he invented more nice things to say. While *not* allowing unwanted sentiments or speculations to intrude. (The mattresses: were they to absorb his blood? Gabe's killing room? Would it be first-degree murder? Or only second: what with Marx having demonized landlords in particular, referring to them as "parasites," the worst grade of capitalist. Had Zeke come across as a landlord sympathizer?)

After a little, our mouse politely gave an excuse and walked across the floor. But then at the street door, well away from Gabe, a slight undertone of anger leaked into his voice as he

Prelude

boldly refused an offered copy of Gabe's latest pamphlet lying on a table there.

It seemed as if Gabe wished to know how far away, for Zeke, the influence of his knife carried. Would a sword/pen combination prove mightier than his pen alone? That, or Zeke had snowed him more than he thought. He drew the latch, the door opened, and down a few stairs was a sidewalk with witnesses. Zeke breathed deeply as he strode swiftly away. What a relief! End of another close shave for 007.

His take on Gabe as a man of action with substantial police anxieties had been more intriguing than disturbing to a mouse of Zeke's limited sophistication and commonsense. But also, when touched on earlier, there seemed good cause for skepticism about his being in prison long. It sounded too much like propaganda after Gabe let drop that he'd been held as a political prisoner but then declined to reveal the precise charge. (That with his over-liberal usage of such terms as "lackeys of imperialism," "Fascists," and "Wall Street bloodsuckers.")

A few years thereafter, though, the mandatory prison tests of cruel and unusual behavior modification drugs, such as Prolixin, came out. They were done upon California inmates by such government agencies as the FBI, CIA, and Pentagon "Intelligence." Bodily aches and a "short fuse" were given as typical examples of their unforeseen chronic side effects. Then should he credit Gabe being imprisoned for his political views? Or, strictly speaking, did he only qualify as a "political prisoner" as soon as he was singled out for compulsory drug

Prelude

testing from a database of incarcerated criminals also caught up in radicalism? Arguably, he sort of did so qualify, if the latter were so.

The evening before the day of their main event, Gabe and he were among a scattered audience in a San Francisco Conservatory of Music recital hall. When the program finished, Gabe praised the pretty female pianists' technique and feeling for Mozart. He asked if Zeke didn't agree. Next, with the small auditorium all but empty, Gabe asked him to wait and went down front. To congratulate her, he said. But soon after he got there, the pianist began shouting at him in a rage. "How dare you come here?" may have been the gist of it—anyway, the only phrase heard clearly. After which came a lower-volume torrent of harsh speech. Then one of her women friends or teacher, and then a male stagehand joined the confrontation.

Gabe retreated back up the aisle. The pianist came behind him and, tears in her eyes, overwrought, denounced Zeke for being his friend. Cried out at him, as he arose, that he should be ashamed of himself. Then spun and hurried down to the stage again without saying more. Tarred with the same brush! When asked about it as they left, Gabe gave only a wry grin.

There and then, Zeke supposed the scene was no more than an aftershock from a nasty divorce and let it go. But after Gabe turned on him, he emerged as more ex-con than agitator. Was this last of the red-hot Marxists a radical robber of banks (all capitalist) to liberate funds for the upcoming revolution? Was that what he went down for?

Prelude

But rather, Zeke had a hunch that it was a deed more along the lines of assault with a deadly weapon, date rape, or possibly murder that put him in the big house. Further, he surmised the only reason he was invited to the recital then was to fill in as a silent henchman sitting many rows back for a probable face-off. There to be a witness while Gabe met his former victim or her pal out in the open. In case she or a friend went berserk, his role for Zeke was to back a plea of self-defense in court, or to be pointed out as an ally.

Be that as it may, one of Gabe's nonpolitical issues, some bad habit, led to hard time in jail and to the pain left over from his abuse there as a lab rat. Maybe actual paranoia was also implicated. (Hostility, suspicion, delusions of radical grandeur?) Although the Prolixin program may have quickened it big-time by temporarily providing his mental state with an inescapable basis in fact. While a third issue of his, or only another indication of paranoia, was severe homophobia—from prison or the streets of San Francisco. He may have been off some schizo medication. But from Zeke's perspective, under the knife, Gabe's main overall problem was violence.

He wasn't so bad, otherwise. What jazz he came out with stayed in tune and rhythm. An ear for music, he had. Plus, regardless of his musicianship, he achieved at least eccentricity in his busking and upside-down yoga asana. What's more, he was idealistic and committed to social improvement, though by unsavory methods. Then there was his mind's superb information storage, too. All in all, quite a superior rat—he'd give him that.

Oh, yes, he was one—never forget the Futurist manifesto! (An influential document for selling an avant-garde art style

Prelude

of old to a more skeptical world.) Some artists and craftsmen *are* rats. At least coming on as such, rock musicians thrive, those professional wrestlers of song. On the other paw, the very capitalist businessmen whom socialists most love to hate may indeed be rats. And the Secret Service must be a rats' nest. Some rats like to justify their murderous urges by making them part of a war effort: a revolution, a cold one, a jihad, any will do.

Then there are rats who totally ignore standards. The majority of male convicts, odds-on, are rats. (Including non-violent offenders other than drug abusers or DUI.) And some will blame God for their bloody mindset. Muslem terrorists are rats, or under their sway. All on their own, though, some rats bloat into charismatic secular gods. Infamous rat tyrants abound. Ivan the Terrible, for the glory of Russian Orthodox Christianity, is said to have tortured about 15,000 subjects. He arose at 4 a.m. daily for three hours of bashing his bean on the floor while prostrated in prayer. Stalin's turn came later. It was said that Hitler's photographic memory helped his speeches persuade.

What struck Zeke about Gabriel was that nothing he said turned out to be as thought-provoking as his way of saying—or more so of misbehaving. Hollywood loves rats. Zeke would have sooner met up with him on film, not live. Although here was somebody in the flesh who could literally speak volumes, the bookish phrases he mostly repeated were uninspiring. He'd memorized obsolete political or economic analysis, not poetry. If only the proletariat could upgrade their scripts, comrade!

Prelude

Not that Zeke's own talk was much. Occasionally, arguing with a contentious rodent, his mighty struggle to come up with some concept on the spot clarified it—anyhow, to his own way of thinking. But that same net result or more could also be had while solitary: from introspecting, study, reconsidering things overheard, or wordless contemplation of things casually seen. So that, generally, he kept busy enough running into himself, vicarious selves, and an occasional large object. He disliked making either conversation or arguments more than most rodents.

Yet, when first finding his way as a rover, our boy Zeke, while in the grip of some unusual togetherness enthusiasm, would try and explain his motivation for carrying on through America by saying that he did it because meeting up with friendly new folks while on the road was easier. Was it? Perhaps so while still inexperienced enough to often be intrigued by fresh random encounters. While he was closer to childhood? But he never solved this enigma. Whether home or away, friendship was infrequent, so he invariably forgot to keep score and compare.

Natural beauty: after his maturing sensibility to it flowered in the open air, the next thing Zeke knew, he had a primary liking for one distinct type. A subdivision of beauty apart, within its misty definition. "Wilderness," they called it. Although, by the time Zeke touched down on Earth, mostly this referred to uncultivated lands with few roads or other constructions upon them. Approximate wilderness, then: remoter territory with footways through it. Tranquil as heaven on Earth, mostly, your earthly concerns far away. Many others were finding it to their liking, too. He had a theory.

Aside from the shattered silence and so forth in rural areas from mechanization, the cultural shift of prevailing taste away from tameness in outdoor settings may have been induced mostly by the sheer scarcity of wilderness. For paintings of the Middle Ages, when they had in their background trees, hills, and so on, normally portrayed cultivated countryside with villages or Arcadian parkland. They omit forests, mountains, or coast. As if back then, well before 19th-century Romanticism, uninhabited upcountry and seashore was too commonplace in Europe to arouse much wordless contemplation. From that more than from seeming, to most artists back then, to be the home of evil; too hostile and fraught with danger to trouble with.

Scarcity more than fear could explain why rougher, wilder landscapes were visible in Chinese art much earlier, by the 6th century. Keeping pace with more rapid destruction of virgin land, due to China's greater population density and flatter terrain. There, too, as lack of wilderness spread, its spiritual significance soared in the eyes of devout artists, monks, and philosophers.

Anywhere, as pasture and cultivated acreage expand and backcountry shrinks, the wilds increase their potency for inspiring aesthetic affect. They gather novelty value. But the quiet pleasure or awesomeness of inviolate nature also derives from its associations, both in space and time. For instance, to all but surrealists, a waterfall looks and resounds best embraced by other odds and ends of nature rather than by a farm, much less an airport. Man-made constructions and noise break its atmosphere. Small parks, farmland, and gardens are also much sought-after, no doubt, but more for convenience, security, sustenance—less for evoking awe. And wilderness goes back further in time, also. It imparts the resonance of primitive eras, and has an authentic feel. (Even where the present-day habitat is an aftergrowth of old-time agriculture.)

"For their timeless originality and understated harmony, calm uninhabited areas look finer to me now than farm country or gardens do. Their variety and complexity goes beyond the artificial. Tangled branches, irregular mountains, twisting streams, elaborate coral reefs—where would I be without those to discuss? I'd have to talk shop, as usual." So some long-winded mouse might, glancing, have said to his or her companion in a squad of hiking mice and guinea pigs last Sunday in some national park.

Back to Zeke, now, from whoever that was, chattering down the footpath. Surely it was no speech act of his. He being more a thinker than a talker. And for him, quiet and privacy went with such subtle delights as woodland like Swiss cheese did with crackers. To Zeke, what natural beauty was out there was as self-evident as lunch and demanded his single-mindedness. Now and again, it could make him squeak for joy and laugh.

To rediscover oneself in surprising, out-of-the-ordinary loveliness outside felt grand. Which emotional coloring could then transform itself into a sunny judgment about life-as-we-know-it, and about the way things were going for him, Zeke.

Prelude

Such territory gave a sense of being in the right place at the right time and wanting things to go on and be as they were.

So-so scenery could even turn him on, with enough desire for walking or swimming in his heart. Indulging his boyish visual trail curiosity about what lay round curves in nature came first. Yet it was the recognition and then penetration of an unmistakably well-pronounced seat of beauty that really got his juices flowing.

Although Zeke's big romance for much of his natural life was with Mother Nature, he also lusted after names on maps. Which is why riding a far ways o'er the map went along with his walking, skin diving, boating, cycling, and other pieces of the action. True, he most desired her afoot but also had pleasure motoring her highways in regions where the trail-hiking possibilities were too pedestrian to consider or nonexistent. He liked wheels, wasn't too bothered by flying, and could put up with boats of all sizes. So that claiming he was in need of globe-trotting to access unique "beauty spots" worldwide, a quest for fabulous localities overseas—that may have been no more than a handy rationalization. Although it *did* seem close enough to verity when he was standing in one. Still and all, he was as much a wanderer as a lover of beauty or misfit hiding in the woods.

That being so, then, what did pure transit do for him? Why did Zeke so take to the road? Might his continuing eagerness for going away derive from suspenseful contingencies of reinforcement, a regular search for irregular rewards—for example, foreign cuisines? (Though a mouse must query whether Skinner's behaviorism, based upon pigeon or rat stimulus-response, can apply to other rodents.) As that may be, Zeke *did* look upon himself more as a mouse in a mess than as a legitimate aesthete, sniffing out eternal elegance with his nose in the air. He being one for whom itinerancy was made engrossing as much by unfamiliarity and obstacles as by natural or artificial prodigies. And though there came delightful scenes, more time was spent in the intervals to and from such places.

"Beauty": to him that indicated anything at all that, when perceived at a distance, brought on pleasant feelings or moods. "At a distance": ruling out tactile pleasure, gustatory pleasure, and conceivably other close-up pleasures unforeseen or forgotten at this time in history. Moreover, sensibility of beauty varies much among individuals, and its labeling or description is also much swayed by convention. Or so they all say.

In whatever way, Zeke managed to acquire an aesthetic opinion or two along his halting way. He even liked to believe he had some new thoughts of his own on the topic. For example, it's only on the periphery of beauty, whether in nature or art, that pure novelty may assist. It draws the curious. But novelty functions only as an introduction to magnificence, as a secondary aspect—not the whole show. The value of exoticism is overrated if it's regarded as the essence of aesthetic pleasure, in the Romantic mode. Contrived novelty is also overrated in the deified newfangledness of modern art. For novelty is no more—though no less—than a condiment to those who feast upon beauty. Although it may perk up flavor, a little can go a long way.

Prelude

Travel can go a long way. It gets some of its zest from sampling unexpected things and those not easily recognized. As it does from minding things that divert and quicken stagnant streams of consciousness. Uncommon things, massive things, stirring things, ever-changing things, bright and shiny things, rackety things, smelly things, tasty things. About anything awakening the senses is better than nothing new. So then, novelty alone may appeal at first.

Simple unpredictability in your current of events is better than nothing, too. And to live at no fixed address dependably has that. Though mingled with stress, if there comes too big a portion of the unpredictable. Casually to be called "adventure," once you're well out of it. (And after its dainty offshoot appears: a lasting reminiscence). Even so, travel adventure most often occurs on a scale and divided by interims that make it tolerable to most.

No tougher than Zeke felt vagrancy more rewarding than not, for a few months at a stretch. Although the hitches and discomforts in getting somewhere *did*, now and then, motivate our oversensitive loner to ask himself whether it was worth it. Packed in his internal baggage, however, was a customary easing idea, all set for precisely such bothersome passages and humors. "Making a trip always tops living in a rut, one day much the same as the next. Definitely beyond where that gets so stale and repetitive that your surroundings turn off, it does. For here in outland, on the move, tomorrow is another day on the way, and things will be seen to change."

Prelude

Susceptibility to boredom, tension in reverse, was part of what drove Zeke onward. (And so continues, to his probable doom, by the way.) Putting it positively, he was out there for the exhilaration of exploration and fresh happenings. His nomadic urge originating in a curious craving for something else. "The profound, enduring intuition that way out *that way*, toward the horizon, lies a reality wonderful, content, and free of tedium." That was the utmost he could describe it.

Howsoever it was that his nomadic urge originated, his wavering feel for the goodness of thither and yon would hustle him forward three or four months on the road. Then the mystery of faraway shores faded, and he went home. ("Home" being city apartments, hotels, or travel-trailers in the U.S. hinterlands.) But then, after about another half year, his land of make-believe reappeared. Only an abnormal enthusiasm for a certain type of activity yields enough energy to invent a routine for oneself, and then follow it—over and over and over there.

My old travel acquaintance, Zeke, at some bright and early juncture in his ramblings got the idea of writing in the travel genre. To that end, he'd try doing what literary journeymen commonly do. Noting where it's at, he'd recklessly make the scene where outlandish what's-its-names were said to flourish, or showpieces of verbal intercourse come to pass. Sadly, it must be said that Zeke was no great shakes as either an adventurer or a jet-setter. He made more than his share of irritating mistakes.

In the end his main project became a concise how-to-do-it booklet for independent budget world-travelers—well short of a memoir. Zeke's little booklet, The Dummy's Guide

Prelude

to Travel and Life, was a runaway bestseller. Its instructions for sleeping, eating, moving, and so on have become a classic in the literature. So much so that a collection of them are presented in this volume. (See Appendix 1.)

Zeke had always wanted to be taken seriously as a writer, but he realized that instruction manuals or how-to booklets are problematic as literature. Is it only because they omit or downplay the horrid consequences of ignoring their recommendations? Right: they gloss over just what may happen! To his way of thinking, Zeke saw that his own useful pamphlet could be enriched through expounding the bungles and occasional happy foresights contributing to its preparation.

He suspected, though, that producing such a thing was outside his own literary forte. Accordingly, it was given to me, the only biographer whom he knew, to explore all the fatigue, discomfort, trifling care, chagrin, self-reproach, frustration, distress, and worse evils that may befall from incorrect touristry. The recurring condition of being there, and being wrong! By explicating that, our collaboration bids fair to make still more "dummies" acquainted with his award-winning travel tips.

Unfortunately, from a biographical standpoint, Zeke, through much of his life, kept to himself. He made few friends, and brought forth scarcely any high-quality talk. His main consolation was in not wasting anything good on impermanence or strewing oral litter, as he thought of it. But a character who didn't say much—a scriptwriter's or novelist's worst nightmare! Even for Zeke's biographer, the only technical literary solution feasible was in adopting a form of

Prelude

author-omniscient point of view—limited third person. I, myself, had to pick through and report Zeke's thoughts, with him so quiet and hard to interview.

The heroic intellectual to whom I wished to play Boswell was of the loquacious Samuel Johnson mold—right there with a reliable stock of pithy quotes. ("The only end of writing is to enable the readers better to enjoy life, or better to endure it." —Samuel Johnson) Lacking a subject so richly aphoristic in his utterances can be a handicap for any biographer, in spite of his craft—not that I'm complaining. Anyway, I've filled in with a few epigraphs by others than Zeke to lighten things up, and satisfy those readers with an appetite for stuff in quotation marks.

Before getting into more of that, though, here is an illustration of what Zeke, on his own, would never say aloud, only think:

> Those entranced novelists who quote characters at length have a special heart's desire to flesh out disguised dialogues of their own, to make them more agreeably apropos. Conversational wish fulfillment is what they're about. Also, they desire completion for the minor, interrupted plot twists of their daily existence. These they also mend with their colorful fabrications, feeling compelled to decorate artless living with ideal finishing touches and what ought to be. (Or moral ambiguity in the best.) Only like that may they shield themselves from the glaring incoherence of their own sober reality. Then, too, left from a lonely childhood may be a preoccupation

Prelude

with the secret thoughts, cozy chats, and love affairs of others. Childish regrets and curiosity complicated by existential anxiety brings out fiction.

Now I ask you! Zeke takes a lot for granted, not having known any such writers more intimately than through their writings. And where's his degree in psychology? Speaking of which, the maladjustment of some wannabe travel *nonfiction* writers, not unlike Zeke, may be even farther round the bend. *Theirs* a preoccupation with inanimate objects—flora and fauna, architecture—or peoples in general more than with concrete identities. Thus, to render their books readable for devotees of fiction and others, they seek to portray and put on the map their own private deeds along with mention of striking peculiarities in landscapes, ethnicities, and so on. Trusting that allowances will then be made for any sketchiness in characterizations and sparse dialogue.

In consequence of which, people pop up and down in their narratives as so often they do for real—fleetingly, poorly observed, without saying much. Which is what such word painters must put up with rather than stretch or fill out characters and turns of events to fit their own imaginings; making what factually came about more satisfying as drama. But is the ongoing plain truth of a journey stimulating enough so that, for any other than the journeyer, it holds interest?

Guidebooks so discriminating as to divulge both where to go and exactly how to get there without making a fool of yourself are uncommon. Also offered throughout this account of one journey among his wide travels are his now-official

Prelude

designations of the most scenic or otherwise mind-blowing spots in Mexico—with their original rating symbols. These resurrected from his travel diaries by this biographer. Ones in which he noted overwhelming undercurrents of: (1.) Happiness. Not-wanting-to-leave; (2.) Nostalgia. A yearn-to-return. This information alone, even more than his former position as U.S. Secretary of Travel, earned him this biography.

Those place names or routes <u>underlined</u> were spots or strips rich in beauty. While those with "(!!!)" after them were others surprisingly high in novelty value or wildlife, but no better than average in the beauty department. Sometimes particular sites, on their own, within cities that were not especially commendable in their entirety are rated as above.

When it came to noting the particulars of anyplace on his itinerary lacking in appearance or ambiance, he seldom bothered. Ordinary locales not underlined or exclamation-pointed by Zeke may have inspired him with assorted thoughts, feelings, or practical lessons, but did not inspire him with the thought or feeling that they were one of the most lovely or novel to behold on earth. So he may have put down their place-listings mainly to remind him, later, where not to return. Anyway, he rarely recorded much in the way of aesthetic detail in these.

Nowadays, having been honored for his achievements in office, Zeke is far beyond caring how he used to be perceived in his wayward youth. Accordingly, in his retirement, he has resolved to bask in the ultimate luxury of celebrity: that of exposing the naked truth about his life and times to the public at large. A "nudism of the inner man", as he once put it. And

Prelude

for the purity of this endeavor, he has the undying respect of his colleagues, family, fellow citizens: of all who know him. A humble ex-public-servant, beloved by all, including this writer.

Tragically, there was a side to Zeke unknown to the general public until now. Another result of our collaboration has been in telling that which few life stories have dared. The sorrows and odd triumphs of a decrepit hippie, often under the influence, and that over a mild attention deficit disorder, complicated by obsessive-compulsiveness, and dissociative fugue. A barely functioning schizoid doing his all, but always suffering from what he should have done on top of what he did. His sorrows and odd triumphs here revealed through slices of his daily life too humiliating, too petty, too weird, too inescapable to be more than hinted in humane letters.

Warning: For stay-at-homes, or folks with excess money, most of Zeke's practical advice may be unhelpful. While it may be necessary for most users of Zeke's travel tips to modify a few—on the basis of their own contradictory hands-on experience or self-knowledge. Besides, such particulars as gender, strength, sophistication, or contingencies in central Africa could also make other revisions desirable. Moreover, though pursued to the letter, most of his advisements only deliver the goods mostly. Therefore, neither Zeke, nor the author, nor the publisher of this text are responsible for, nor assume any liability for undesirable outcomes from the use of Zeke's tips. (Although only taking a quick peek at Appendix 1 wouldn't hurt.)

Parenthesized reference numbers in the following text—**(50)** etc.—refer to the Appendix. To speed scanning for

Prelude

relevant solutions, likely limits to applicability on the basis of two differentials are provided: (1.) their general location—(Foreign) or (Domestic); (2.) approximate stage of economic development—(Modern) or (Developing). Those not prefaced by any of these four terms should apply equally well almost anywhere. ("Domestic" refers to North America, and the offshore states or provinces of the U.S. and Canada. "Foreign" to all other countries.)

Many of these solutions have Exceptions (in parentheses). Some have exceptions with the same terms of limitation, based on location or economics, as entire solutions do. In which case, these terms refer only to the sentence that they immediately precede. Additionally, some solutions are followed by brief explanations [in brackets.]

MEXICO

Most of the cities and towns here are only points of reference for less-populous areas of beauty or novelty named in the text, and shown on more detailed maps.

MEXICO

- San Luis Potosi
- Pachuca
- Papantla
- San Miguel de Allende
- Guanajuato
- Tlaxcala
- Xalapa
- Morelia
- Queretaro
- Mexico City
- Puebla
- Amecameca
- Veracruz
- Cuernavaca
- Villahermosa
- Palenque
- San Cristobal de las Casas
- Oaxaca
- Chiapa de Corzo
- Huatulco

Trip 1
(October–December 1983)

Mexicali—Chihuahua—Creel

Zeke crossed at Mexicali. This, his first Mexican vagrancy, was only his second into the Third World. Forsooth, foreshadowed by Morocco, where a noisome amoebic dysenteric end befell a callow Zeke upon his ill-starred hippie endeavor at circling the whole Earth overland. From Luxembourg's wintry blast, his pilgrimage wended its merry way, by thumb, to the orange-scented coasts of sunny Spain and sailed the Gibraltar Strait. Whence the fabled express train bore him to Marrakesh. A mere fortnight thereafter, alas, his passage through Muslim territory discovered its end of the Earth, and what it was to be seriously bummed out, on a secondhand bicycle not far beyond a vile village well in the arid hinterland northeastward.

After those giddy days, while going about in North America, Zeke got more into hiking than biking. Hence, Mexico came to be his first developing country featuring trail-walking. A fresh departure into the radical madness of far-out foreign travel, as he liked to think of it then.

Mexico: Trip 1

Mexicali, city of prefab name and fame. There Zeke first penetrated the confines of exotic Mexico—only to find a mess of derelict, modernistic shelters. With a peculiar, desolated air about many, as if not regularly lived in. Where *was* everybody? Anyway, there *he* was, suffocating in squalid heat, diesel fumes, more heat, noise, and dense brown smog—even by L.A. standards, a nasty urban waste. Suffering culture shock and itchy-jock, a sweaty Zeke boarded the soonest southbound train.

Then his long stroll to a viable seat commenced. Through cars of boozy boozers, exploding in full-throated words and laughs. Through cars of mothers with screaming babies. On past seats near car ends, stinking potently of urine from nearby toilet closets. While the air conditioning weakened the farther to the rear from the engine he walked, giving out entirely after three or four cars. After which, he turned back to only his next-best seat—his first choice, by then occupied. Thus he learned, more than when boarding a bus, choosing an unreserved train seat is a matter of elimination. (Except on trains so jampacked that any vacant seat attracts.) **(1)**

Creel—Barranca del Cobre Nat. Pk.—Batopilas

He got off near the rim of Copper Canyon. "Really, a system of several canyons," it says here. "And deeper than the Grand Canyon of Arizona," his guidebook went on to say. But less colorful than Grand Canyon, it was. In most sections, as seen from above, less sheer and rocky, too. Its slant admitting a blotchy layer of green vegetation, distantly gray. Though

Mexico: Trip 1

gashed by substantial cliffs of pale yellow-cream-white lava. With mostly pine woods up high. Cedar. Yucca.

Zeke wandered for days on dirt roads through the gaping world about him, down small valleys and through forests south of Creel. Going by Tarahumara Indians farming with hand tools, dressed in spiffy costumes. Men wearing short white skirts, and billowy white shirts with full sleeves, and dangling red headbands. Some were barefoot, and some wore sandals with leather thongs wrapping their ankles. Women wore long dresses, long-sleeved blouses, and headscarves, all in bright-colored prints. Living in both converted caves and huts of wood and fieldstone, they were.

Zeke afterwards learned, in their version of Catholicism, that non-Indians are children of the Devil. Forasmuch as Satan is God's brother, after death all non-Tarahumara who haven't been too wicked go to a relatively pleasant zone of Hell. One separate from Tarahumara Heaven, though. It explained why they always kept their distance from him there below.

Going down to Batopilas, the twisty-turny, one-lane dirt road followed a mountain ledge without guardrails. Inches of dust divided the beat-up bus from a lot of thin air. Although in some portions of the long switchback, its tires tracked wheel ruts either worn or dug—an historical carriageway? Zeke was sorely fretted. Only the placid presence of folksy passengers and the driver's careless expression kept him from asking to get off at one of its leveler turns, and walk down.

The town at the bottom was where all bandits in westerns riding for the border wound up, if they got away. Authentic

Mexico: Trip 1

to a fault, with farm animals in the cobbled streets outnumbering cars: turkeys, pigs, horses. An inhabited, flat-fronted western film-set, the canyon its time portal. With Spanish ornamentation like window grilles, and with no boardwalks, to look more Mexican.

Its environs felt deep-sunk and remote; sliver of another century caught in a cranny. After a while, downriver, Zeke prowled jungle shambles of an old hacienda, partially overrun with high, magenta bougainvillea. Batopilas was formerly one of the largest silver-mining towns in Latin America.

He awoke in his tent—up top again—a considerable walk from Creel. Having previously asked the departure time of the bus to the Basaseachic Falls turnoff, though, he knew there was a fair chance of making it, moving right along. But the scenery ambushed him. It made him want to go slow. And so, out of patience with his own tendency for timeliness, he made the untimely assumption there would also be a later bus departure than the one he knew. Thereby he granted himself the leisure to explore a promising side canyon with mushroom-shaped entrance rocks, glimpsed a short ways back at dusk.

It proved a disappointment. In morning light, the rocks outcropped less strikingly. Afterwards, making town extended his disappointment. Not only had rock fairyland failed to materialize, once in town, he stumbled into a harsh one-bus-per-day reality. It had gone. Things just weren't working out for him. Zeke, you cockeyed optimist, quit supposing unknown bus schedules liberal with departures. **(2)(3)(4)**

Mexico: Trip 1

Suffering chagrin, he brooded:
>Thanks to a nearly continuous flow of small practical worries, failures, complications, and temporary discomforts, travel mostly keeps attention pinned to the near future. To the here and now it does only in really curious, ominous, or beautiful surroundings, of unpredictable occurrence. Well, being pressured to live primarily in travel's more typical time frame, one jump ahead of the present, yields far from ideal mental functioning. For the totally enlightened mind would constantly experience a calm absorption in immediacy while ignoring that which may or may not come hither shortly along its way. Walking sudden Zen enlightenment: Now!
>
>Didn't click again . . . And yet, even my near-future brainwork in transit gives some relief from a bad habit of dreamy other-day, other-place inattention. My thinking on the go lets perception slide, on average, less out of focus than did thinking while at ease on familiar ground. Travel does oblige a minor adjustment, at least, down to a more short-range field of view.

You see, Zeke was one of those mice with a milder sort of attention-deficit disorder who stared out the window while enduring school classes. Onward in his career, though, he began wearing corrective travel lenses and spent much of his adulthood beyond the pane. Long days beneath the wheeling sun, a poet might say. Although, near as often, studying changes of scenery while gazing out fresh windowpanes at speed. Any child whose eye stays always on the ball indoors may overlook their window of opportunity through mobility—lackaday—and won't grow up to be a vagabond.

Creel—<u>Cascada de Basaseachic Nat. Pk</u>

Anyhow, that bonus day in Creel could have gone worse. ("Seeing that it had more local color and fewer outsiders than now," a travel snob might complain.) Then, next day, the bus brought him to a certain village, and from there he rode a pickup truck some way out to the cascade. His first long-distance cab ride ever: instant status! Through a wasteland where thumbing might be unwise for sundry reasons, among them the affordability of truck fare.

Third-highest waterfall in North America, some say. In any event, putting all statistics aside for the next nine pages or more, a tall one. Whose flying plume, at their approach, way-off, had an alluring glitter, like a colossal drinking fountain encircled by desert. A high geyser of water, rather than a fall, it seemed.

They got there early, to a plunging trail from a little-used road. Zeke went partway down. Below, a white heavy mist floated in a dun and beige cliff amphitheater. Black rock mottled green backed the fluid column; falling water wrapped in mist where it struck below. And there, out from liquid's grand impact on liquid, a doe and fawn grazed on a green grassy and wet boulder islet, fading in and out through the windblown white.

Mexico: Trip 1

Creel—Railroad to El Fuerte—Los Mochis—Mazatlan—Tepic

On the train to Tepic, Zeke couldn't help meeting another American: Paul. An extrovert who asserted, among other things, that train rides were "good for meeting people." A self-described "refugee from Detroit," looking to settle in Argentina. His last job was supervising a photo processing lab. Glib, confident, smiley, medium height, mesomorphic, fair-skinned, handsome. His first name was that of a boyhood pal. (Another crew-cut guinea pig who joined the Navy, relocated to San Diego, got married, and then committed suicide.)

After they got off for a brief sip of atmosphere at Tepic, Zeke made known what his next destination would be. Then Paul, who followed no itinerary, tagged after him off the arid plateau and down to a green tropical shore.

San Blas

They shared a hotel room. Paul, who had Spanish, hung out in the plaza that evening, chatted with some natives, bought some weed. While Zeke went to bed about ten, as was his wont. Paul being more nocturnal.

In the prime of the morning, Zeke ambled the streets unaccompanied. Seeing riotous tropical verdure in vacant lots, the overgrown ruins of both a cathedral and modern government building, pigs indulging themselves in a side street, droves of poor and dirty children running and squealing, a forgettable beach, and a salt marsh with mosquitoes. The air was odorous and moist, like a soft weight pressing

Mexico: Trip 1

him. This, his first tropical Latin American town, made a sinister impression. The locality bore a pervasive fragility-of-civilization ambience, beneath a rotting vegetation smell. With jungle slipping back to drag all human habitation down into the primordial hog wallow.

Near high noon at the hotel, Zeke felt inclined to move on to Puerto Vallarta. Although Paul, recently out of bed, liked where they were. "A place to slow down after too many days of train riding." Thus he tried persuading Zeke to stay over, but didn't. "Mostly I prefer traveling solo," he said. *How could I have said it nicer?* our semi-tactful mouse thought to himself as Paul, looking miffed, left the room. But Zeke even then considered them to be on a fair footing.

From past trips he knew:

> The outdoor games I like best are solitary—including overland journeys on both roads and trails. The immediacy of others disrupts my enjoyment of all such activities—maybe excepting old, old companions. Definitely strangers or recent acquaintances do. To others detected by any sense, my brain reacts with thoughts on my identity, their identity, or society. Usually, with too-familiar thoughts which make perceptions of my environment intermittent. Hence, for me the presence of others cannot be disregarded in predicting an outdoor game's worth, whether high or down. In contrast, concentration on precisely what I'm doing and where I'm at *does* produce enjoyment. Forgetting myself, along with any surrounding selves, yields happiness.

Mexico: Trip 1

Zeke took a shower and then had lunch. After, going to pay, he noticed a 500 peso note (about $20) was missing from his wallet. Meantime, Paul had packed and quit the hotel. $20 for *one joint?!*

Zeke had comparable misadventures with other rebuffed rodents in both the U.S. and U.K. Some guinea pig or rat would glam onto him, usually in a city, and begin stringing along while bringing round Zeke to, instead, tag after *him*. Zeke's gentle demeanor, scrawniness, ostensibly kind disposition, and sense of humor persuaded them of his value as a goofy sidekick. They expected admiration from a guy like him, though, instant friendship, possibly a loan or a few beers, too. But then, snubbed!

"I vant to be alone," wasn't good enough. Some were difficult to ditch. When his obstinate streak revealed itself, they often took a small revenge, like stealing some item before parting. One attempted extortion. They deemed a reluctance to be bossed from a less virile man, upon whom they had expended some amount of personality, as disrespect. As that may be, male dominance behavior no longer got him down so often as it had in early youth. And, progressively, their interpretation of his standoffishness grew more accurate. Beyond merely a sensitive loner's taste for solitude and freedom, in him there arose a streak of disrespect, blended with distrust, for the pushier members of his gender.

As it turned out, that first Mexican sightseeing trip, Zeke encountered no indigenous thieves. A second jaunt also gave the impression that Mexicans living their folkways were honest toward outsiders. Except now and then in a few hangouts

Mexico: Trip 1

that saw a good many travelers, such as big city bus terminals. On his third journey, though, in '02, things showed signs of rapid deterioration. Drugs, guns, and media programming was his guess why.

In the '80s, he was seldom shortchanged. At worst, where he bought nothing, and asked directions to a business rival, he'd get a bum steer. For instance, at a hotel with no vacancies, asking which way to another hotel might result in being set wrong. After being accosted by a cabdriver, asking where the bus to Mexico City stopped might bring the same penalty.

Once a small grocer overheard Zeke suggest looking for a supermarket to an acquaintance and misdirected him without being asked, urging them to go there. Even before Zeke had made up his mind about the box of crackers he was grasping. As he later, more frequently, saw in China and this or that other country, lies involved with trade were the main demonstration of class or race aversions. Up till then, Zeke more often met with a ratty punitive impulse due to his lack of care for unequal friendship.

Up in California, he chanced upon occasional Mexican expats who did not live up to their hardworking and courteous stereotype. Banditos! Particularly untrustworthy they were after staring into his eyes a mite too long, too soon, and then smiling inordinately. The symptoms of those assuming a playfully predatory attitude where they saw weakness. Instinctively making the most of a gentleman unlikely to attack if their theft or lies were detected—up to a point, polite enough, though. But unequal friendships held less interest for them than for white rats. As if pigmentation or class consciousness got in the way.

Down in old Mexico, Zeke was seeing that both guinea pigs and rats, on their home turf, often did excellent Spanish courtly imitations of mousey manners—respectful tones of voice, courteous smiles, gentle handshakes, and so on. As if aiming to project humility and sweetness of temperament to a greater extent than even the best-behaved guinea pigs of his acquaintance bothered with up north. He wondered whether this sort of formal display was due to a more fragile culture, the offshoot of a higher probability of meeting with little-provoked violence from their rat or drunken-guinea pig fellow-citizens in the hot-blooded south. Native American blood mixing with booze to support and preserve old-world gentility!

Indigenous differences in courtesies aside, though, rats the world over identify themselves with violence. That being their principal manly virtue rather than some kind of theft. Although, arguably, the essence of brutality is a taking away from its victim. Crunch! Out flies his tooth. And so, from that perspective, theft, cheating, verbal humiliation and the like might be reckoned as pulled punches. As tactics to vent violence with more discretion, being less incriminating or explicit. Rats, however, are defined by their violence, not their dishonesty. As guinea pigs, or even mice to lesser extent, may also cheat or steal. Only in aggression's most extreme form is health or life threatened.

Guinea pigs in good standing may lapse by responding to some kind of direct threat or dishonesty with brute force: nothing less compelling than that, however. Righteous fury

Mexico: Trip 1

or in defense—and not because they judge it admirable. In the world's present low state, nipping back at an aggressive rat may qualify as community service. Although, no doubt, it be chiefly done for self-affirmation. Even daring to speak about such things may represent another excusable style of defensive aggression. **(5)**

Puerto Vallarta

Zeke was tramping out to the edge of town along a beachside road, seeking a hidden overnight camp. When, at the base of a long hill, a group of Mexicans sitting and lying in the shade, close to the roadway, beckoned him to join them and take it easy. Stupid grins, and one held out a bottle. "Come! Join our abandoned bacchanal!" he might have said, for all Zeke knew. Gringo mouse paused for breath-catching and effect, return-smiled, and then gave a believable rendition of "I don't speak Spanish," with egregious mispronunciation. "HAHAHAHAHA!" they went. He did a shrug and grin for encore. Exit up the hot hill, under his ridiculous backpack.

Ignorance of foreign languages can be beneficial, even indispensable upon occasion. From pure habit, a deceptive speaker of perfect Spanish might have delivered the same with correct pronunciation and thereby undermined its effect.

Although drinking from a nearly full bottle may awhile pass for a ceremonial rite of fellowship—even a chance to be a real man among men—the outcome of grog in partnership for a Johnny-come-lately often hits bottom when the bottle empties. When dominance demos may then begin to flow.

With one extra-uninhibited macho in the packo, and with no ready excuse for dashing off, underdog Zeke might have had more than a hangover to worry about. (And swilling roadside on the ground *did* look definitely canine, somehow.) **(6)**

Alcohol, not cannabis, stood out or lay about emphatically as Mexico's soft drug of choice. Nearly every restaurant had a bar attached. Bars had bars attached. Cantinas were men-only bars (back then). But with all those stools to keep them in place, there were still casual drunks sliding into prone positions on the streets. *Mañana* had yet to bring everyone automobile seats and gas tanks to fill between bars and glasses.

Puerto Vallarta—Costa Alegre—Tenacatita

Palm-roofed *palpas* sat on the tan beach of a deeply indented bay. Crescents of spiny brown rocks formed low headlands with faraway haze. Brown pelicans leaped into the air from near islands, flew briefly, then folded wings and slumped down like wet towels over fish. Raptors from inland went drifting high above, egrets and cormorants in the drink. An aquamarine ocean was almost warm as bathwater. In the coconut grove, huge land crabs on tiptoe ran sideways in half-circles and then froze, like clockwork chess pieces. The foul smell of muddy mangrove swamp hovered behind the beach. Resplendent orange-red sunsets appeared.

Where the beach bypath met the Jalisco highway, buses did not often stop. Furthermore, Zeke didn't know either when the Guadalajara bus was due or for sure that Mexican buses stopped when flagged. Would any *collectivo* van or taxi speeding the curve and up the hill see him in time to brake?

Mexico: Trip 1

So he waved at nearly everything coming. An overcrowded bus finally rolled to a halt.

The driver asked where he was going. Having read the bus's destination sign before boarding, our gringo mispronounced it, and off they went. Cleverly, he did not say, "Guadalajara." The driver might then have insisted in unassailable Spanish that he step down and be left behind for an eventual direct bus. Instead, Zeke hopped off in some village where that one turned up a side road for the hills. Which proved a passable hitching post. **(7)**

What notions littered Zeke's mind as he stood by the road hitchhiking?

> Same as walking trails or shady rural lanes, hitchhiking retards my sense of wasting time. Yes, it does relax that chronic mode of anxiety somewhat. Unfortunately, my eased sense of duration while thumbing a ride is apt to occur mostly along modern highways—with their traffic noise, hot sun, blighted roadsides, and passing stares. It involves unpleasantness akin to a telemarketing job—from being seen briefly at a distance, however, rather than distantly heard.
>
> Besides, hitchhiking, for me, entails a self-imposed deadline, though one from which hurry or worry cannot aid rescue. Someone must stop within the 45 minutes I've allotted them. After which I will either try somewhere else or quit for the day, according to my standard procedure.

Mexico: Trip 1

Only after getting a ride and then getting off somewhere I want does hitching lose its bothersome undercurrent of uncertainty. Or, if nobody stops, and I decide to call it a day, a mood of frustration may arise. Enough to negatively affect my morale even the following morning. So, actually, thumbing is not all that soothing as a form of transportation. Unless I methodically drink beer beforehand. Taking a bus is nearly always preferable if it goes where you want.

Barra de Navidad—Guadalajara—Zacatecas—San Luis Potosi—Pozos

There was a footpath to a mining ghost town: Pozos. When coming back, he came face to face with a squinty-eyed, fierce-looking youth—a probable rat. Who used his few words of English plus vigorous gestures to bring Zeke to a standstill. At which Zeke, master of modulation, gave him some adequately relaxed English patter and grinned. Then the typecast juvenile delinquent flashed a grin, too, but his eyes were vivid gonzo. An arrest came to his politeness. He was thinking. Was he measuring the possibility of doing something violent?

They chanced to converge on a narrow ledge trail midway up a steep, barren mountainside of scree and infirm soil. Where, with no assistance from ghost towns, the secret thoughts of a new arrival met eyeball to eyeball were spooky. Perchance only a morbid delusion, but Zeke suspected he saw a series of questions flitting behind the youth's fixed expression. "Is this goggle-eyed gringo carrying anything valuable? Does he have a companion bringing up the rear? Is some local not far behind me? If I hit him with my flashlight, would he take me over the edge with him as he fell?" He was clenching a long, black flashlight that looked heavy. But the situation was fraught with doubt, and so they said "Adios."

There, not having much Spanish had been unhelpful. Coming across as neither visibly nor audibly spooked was the most Zeke could do. A show of fear only encourages evil spirits. But yet, as luck would have it, hiding uneasiness in a tight spot was one of Zeke's specialties. An introspective mind primed with adrenalin aids acting talent in a crisis. (As may a variety of other intoxicants at correct dosage.) The Mexican standoff. **(8)(9)**

Queretaro—Morelia

Morelia cathedral: Inside, musky clouds of incense were afloat, revealing otherwise immaterial, imperceptible air. An immense pipe organ radiated echo pulse. Thoroughly spiritualized was the air. Mouths of children sang out of the transcendent haze—choir practice. Gathered together in a sweet Spanish colonial atmosphere were tokens of the two primary passions of Mexico: religion and reproduction. **(10)**

Uruapan

Eduardo Ruiz Nat. Pk.: Into a glorified city park in Uruapan he strolled, to imbibe flowery tropical flora along shadowed river headwaters with white, bubbly cascades.

Suggesting wonderful childhood gardens in which more flowers were overhead, the air saturated with pungent new odors, the streamlet gurgling, and up the singular way onward lay the completely unexpected.

There she was. Along the creek, heavyset brown females doing laundry. Gauguin would have liked the scene, though none had bare breasts. And the river's residents—fish, amphibians, and all the filthy little insects—got detergent in their mouths if they opened them to complain.

High falls on the opposite side of town, also on parkland, were dominated by trash: plastic bags, plastic jugs, tin cans, broken bottles, garbage, feces with toilet paper. Strength of sensibility in Mexico was enough to create parks, but not quite enough to resist negative urban pressures upon them. Far and wide, insensitivity to natural beauty prevailed, its end result worsened by population density.

To their natural credit, though, out-of-town Mexican parks accumulated fewer of the more permanent artificial eyesores common in their U.S. counterparts: paved parking lots, snack bars and convenience stores, picnic sheds, steel utility shacks, paved trails, concrete footbridges fronting waterfalls, wooden subdivisions for park employees. Mexico's smaller parks had not dwindled into asphalt-lovers' rest stops.

Volcan Paricutin (!!!)

A village buried to partway up its church steeple in lava. Way down south there, nature struck back with pavement of her own. No ordinary war-zone desolation: God's wrath! Could all this fire and brimstone that came down in 1943 be

Mexico: Trip 1

divine retribution for Mexico's role in World War II? Then what about the Mexican War?

Patzcuaro—Zirahuan lake

Have its old buildings alongside peaceful blue water survived buildup since the '80s? Then it was a paradise with quaint buildings amid flowers and foliage: magenta bougainvillea, palms, pale-green willows, water-hyacinth, red hibiscus. A small model of Lago Patzcuaro in its former glory, which was itself, plausibly, a smaller model of Lago Texcoco, altered by Aztec irrigation projects and then sucked dry and buried beneath Mexico City.

Miguel Hidalgo Nat. Pk./Desierto de Los Leones Nat. Pk.

Before Mexico City, Zeke got off the bus for a last gulp of fresh air. Most of three days he ranged the mountains. In the course of which they gave the feel of being too familiar—much like high landscapes in Arizona and New Mexico. The tang of resin in the air, with room to spare among pines and firs with scant undergrowth. Which allowed small cacti, a smattering of deciduous trees, rocks, and more rocks. "I'm seeing a lot of sky through the treetops ahead!": Zeke's favorite hopeful slogan while trudging uphill, anticipating the top.

Villagers weren't up on where trails began or led. There were no blazes, either. Rather a confusing muddle of prominent, narrowish trails, their goals known only to absent woodcutters and herders. Zeke kept to what he took for the main one, going mostly upslope; which abruptly ended, though, without passing viewpoints. So, how it looked, he'd gone off his through trail way back, if there was one. On the way down, another he crossed went over and joined a dirt road.

Slowly upward in low groaned the pickup truck of one friendly park employee. More than happy, he was, to give a ride up to the observatory to which Zeke aspired. Motor vehicles do have their uses. More often than not, though, faring afoot in high terrain without a map or signposts, a mouse with poor sense of direction wastes much energy in getting where he's going. If he ever does. (11)

When camping up high overnight, temperature may replace both uphill work and not tumbling off as paramount problems. Hypothermia gives concern. Although temperature, on average, only falls about 3°F (2°C) per 1000 ft. (300 m.) of elevation gain, there is often added wind chill. To illustrate, Zeke, there in his summer bag, warm enough down to 40°, spent a nearly sleepless night, up a frigid volcano above a hot plateau. As a result, the next day started out sluggish-minded. So that, in his descent, he sat in icky, sticky pine pitch. (12)(13)

Mexico City

Getting topographic maps, Zeke confronted a couple bureaucrats, both with affluent paunches, whose status and job security had them putting on airs. Their's was an unconcealed tone of contempt—slothful contempt, the worst kind. Holding down a government clerical job seemed to be a noteworthy and ego-nourishing gig there in the capital. Maybe their political party had been in power for so long it was sprouting an aristocracy, democracy gone to seed.

Mexico: Trip 1

Outside of that government office, Mexicans were more respectful. Attitudes of superiority were seldom seen. Good manners were. They neither stared at the faces of passersby too long nor openly eyeballed their movements from too close, nor gave more than polite glances. Male civilities to women were observed. More Mexican men were noticeably correct, for whatever reason, than up in Gringoland.

Except in certain situations, that is. For instance, a modern innovation, the automobile, drove them outside their realm of respect. Pedestrians had no rights. Drivers slowed or hit the brake pedal reluctantly if they lagged, at the last moment. Also, base pedestrians, among themselves, might share the same disrespect for the less-powerful as drivers did. The populace, waiting for service somewhere, often crammed to the fore at once rather than take their turns. Mobs of older womenfolk ran "ladies first" into the ground.

Zeke was to come up against these two kinds of bad manners in many developing countries besides Mexico. He had a theory that pushy pedestrian conduct prevails where fewer citizens are much conscious of time slipping away, making the majority routinely less resentful at losing precious minutes to competitive latecomers. Similarly, pushy driving is met with where those who can afford cars are more apt to feel pressed for time than a much bigger bunch, less swayed by the clock, who cannot afford automobiles. Which is why imposing upon widespread patience and calm disregard for duration comes to be the norm with drivers. Two related outcomes of feeble time awareness in the masses: predominantly male-driven cars poking their way through columns of pedestrians at street crossings, and middle-aged matrons elbowing their way through crowds.

An alternative theory, that a weaker respect for personal space on the street accompanies a more robust tolerance or desire for touching strangers, seemed less promising. It might apply to rubbing shoulders, but not to bulldozing bodies with moving bumpers. Even though more such desire for touch may affect standard talking distances.

Once, though, standing erect in the damp warmth of a packed subway car, a shapely woman, without eye contact, deliberately rubbed her torso against Zeke between a few platforms. If a hooker, her tactile brand of advertising had it all over posters on the car walls. In spite of it, mouse that he was, our sappy Zeke felt too shy, cautious, and short on both language and money to initiate a field study on the spot. Why, though, beyond any obvious rationale of just doing her job, rub against his uncomfortably bony physique like that? Could the subway be where girls go wild in Mexico? She was only an anomaly, not a trend, he concluded—an isolated case of frotteurism. Most young ladies in Mexico were decidedly reserved, so far as he could tell.

Physical modesty in public normally goes with a gentler temperament after childhood. In Mexico, the proportion of female mice to female guinea pigs did meet the eye as a little higher than up north; leastways from a distance, and whether or no much of it was pose. But then too, absolute dullness of mind can often be confused with the dreaminess of many youthful mice.

Mexico: Trip 1

Mexico City—Acolman monastery—Teotihuacan ruins (!!!)

Acolman was Spanish Catholic architecture at its heaviest. No more uplifting in its exterior than some boxy up-to-date construction overweight with materialism, its patina of age being its only charm. Additionally, in another Mexican town, which shall remain nameless, Zeke *did* set his critical eye upon an unlovely, late-model, concrete cathedral. Now, Zeke harbored no blind faith that all concrete buildings are ugly. (There was grainy, Roman cement in the Pantheon.) Nor, to Zeke, was the functional stinginess of undecorated angular lines necessarily ugly. Austerity may be okay, even striking, he felt, where isolated by sufficient spacing. Rather, what most made this new cathedral unsightly were the uncomplimentary remnants of an old Spanish colonial church too close; its one upright wall refurbished and protected with a gross plastic roof. The incongruity of building stones and plastic together were obtruded upon by the sad dissonance of a titanic, gray, flat-slab backdrop.

Juxtaposing two distinct architectural styles too close diminishes the impact of both as much as a plastic roof over stone does. Even so, their placement vis-à-vis each other could have born witness to a dead past, rather than merely been tired observance of sacred domain or some zoning law. Was the building complex, in its entirety, supposed to be symbolic? An old skull of a wall, with exquisite stonework framing its hollow window sockets and door maw. That held up as a mask before concrete sins of the Roman Catholic church in its harsh

Mexico: Trip 1

bygone days. Courtesy of a contemporary architect influenced some by Mesoamerican pyramids.

Old-time architecture commonly got the upkeep that it deserved in old Mexico, though. Where, for that matter, preservation obtained for institutions as well as buildings. Only when he got to India and Egypt did Zeke bump up against other republics more temperamentally conservative. There was no denying it—both Jesuits and pyramid builders had descendents living down there.

"... *much fatigue is a product of the subjective conscious mind, and bicameral man, building the ... gigantic temples at Teotihuacan with only hand labor, could do so far more easily than could conscious self-reflective men. ... [Bicameral men were] more alert to visual stimuli, as might be expected if we think of them as not having to strain such stimuli through a buffer of consciousness.*" —Julian Jaynes

About fifty kilometers (thirty-one miles) from Mexico City sat the Pyramids of the Sun and Moon. Inasmuch as they were so close and notable, a throng came out daily to upholster their durability in mutable flesh and clamor. So once again Zeke undertook his strategy for maximum loneness at such sites. Coming soon before dusk, he made a dry camp in a fallow field behind a row of low trees, in proximity to the center of attraction. Then, next morning, he was right there when the gate first opened. He was the first to rise over the Pyramid of the Sun that day! By the time tour buses began arriving about 11 a.m., Senor Speedy Gonzalez was sniffing for green cheese among obscure artifacts over by the Moon. **(14)**

Tramping down the Pyramid of the Sun soon after dawn, Zeke's footfalls echoed off its terraced sides in the silence up there. It thumped like a stone drum. A symmetrical artificial hill, modeled on the barren pyramidal peaks afar, where the gods were also known to dwell. ("World's third largest pyramid," and so forth and so forth a guide might shout in your ear.)

Plunging stone flights induced a stately measured tread. Stairways treacherously steep and shallow, very gradually curving sideways rather than going straight down. Steps so laid being easier to mind, climbing down, from the corner of a raised priestly eye, and also serving to reduce the momentum of descent. In the day when railings either had not been invented, or would offend the gods and architects of round about the year zero. So that any priest back then, meditating upon other than the hardness under his heals, might be prone to plod into emptiness and then bounce and roll downward to the Highway of the Dead far below. For steps and risers lay right before their eyes while climbing up the angled walls connecting narrow terraces, but going down, such was the angle, those flights of stairs had a way of disappearing. Simulated mountaintops might not only ritualize, but also demonstrate through accidents the presence of death in life.

Did the shadowy Indian empire that built Teotihuacan intend it, beyond its ceremonial functions, as a subtle trap to hasten the downfall of any unwary or overconfident citizens? Fewer clumsy, untalented soldiers to feed and instant human sacrifices. Many accidental deaths associated with a sacred structure might only go to increase its mystique and fatal lure. The gods' big, stone killing machine, as it were. The old, the handicapped, the unruly children, and the daydreamers might not be missed by any but underclass family members—decidedly not by the priest-royals. While daredevil athletes might run footraces up and down its sides, apart from ceremonial days: a primitive substitute for drag racing on Sunday. Or was it only a corpulent speed bump on the Highway of the Dead, of which the congregation mostly steered clear?

Notwithstanding, the hard truth that hazardous staircases may have been designed that way may be suspected, from one understood use for an Aztec pyramid at Tenochtitlan in present-day Mexico City. There, after enemy prisoners and others had their living hearts cut out and burned as a sacrifice, their bodies were rolled downstairs. Where below, they turned into tenderized meals for the high-minded, public-spirited, and patriotic citizens whose status merited a non-vegetarian diet. (Or that was one conjecture. A less-dramatic one being that, after heart and head removal, the body was then divided in a more orderly fashion among various nobles and the victim's captor.)

Primeval pyramid builders may have been less dreamy-eyed than us, more like wide-awake jaguars. As if, not having to watch their step, they *were* their step. Minds as detached from worries, regrets, hopes, or old memories as Zen monks in satori. Stray-minded individuals being less common then? Thusly did Zeke descend onto the uncertain footing of Jaynes' bicameral mind.

Mexico: Trip 1

Mexico City

To this day occur many open, unmarked street or sidewalk repair and mystery excavations in Mexican cities. Are safety-warning markers less necessary than up north? Once out walking near the city, Zeke was taking a break, sitting on a hillside in sparse low brush, close above the trail. Where all the Indians going by, whether by themselves or with companions, spied him. Few of the mestizos did, though. (The Mexican population has about six times as many mestizos as Indians.) But in urban surroundings, mestizos may approach the alertness to their habitat legendary for Indians, for all he knew. In that case, had he plunged into some trench where a stretch of sidewalk used to be in Mexico City, no one else might be dropping in on him anytime soon—a few gringos, at most.

Much care about excavation safety may only go to show weakness in a will without adequate machismo. Something which was making Zeke unfit for downtown Mexico City on other accounts, too. For instance, where the rugged city did not jeopardize health with sudden pitfalls, it did insidiously with air pollution and loud noise. Its atmosphere in sunlight was a darker brown than he saw last time in L.A. So that he was repeatedly stunned when he first went out by the weird lighting, smoke, and nerve-shattering racket—as if he were strolling into a vast discotheque just beyond his hotel lobby.

Almost too exciting, it was! But Zeke was then inexperienced enough to put up with it a short while. So much so that he became a contender for the all-time Mexico City touring record by hieing to 34 historic, pre-disco sites in less than a week. After which he reeled for an exit.

Laguna de Zempoala Nat. Pk.—Cuernavaca

Another city, another bus problem. Late afternoon, and we see Zeke boarding the wrong city bus in Cuernavaca. After a mile or so, finding himself in error on the map, he gets off. Then as twilight settles, we take leave of him on a nearly deserted street in an undeniable slum. Lingering there to learn whether the bus downtown or the bandito will arrive first. The bus did. **(15)**

Zeke's regular wayfaring wont was to arise at dawn and then generally get back to a hotel room not long after sunset. And his built-in biorhythmic bed- and wakeup times were not the only reason. Such a regimen had special advantages while bumming around. More privacy at trailheads or tourist magnets, for one; more to be seen looking out of transportation vehicles in daylight for another. But more important in the long run, it often kept him from bumping into rats. Not only in rundown barrios, but everywhere the world over, more rats come out after sundown, rats of all classes.

In the course of a lifespan of nocturnal street, bar, subway, and disco avoidance, odds of skirting open manholes, traffic accidents, assault, robbery, rape, and venereal disease are all improved. As they are against many other dramatic metropolitan misadventures and crimes best seen on a hotel TV—where heroes and heroines mostly win. And yet there are perils on the night-shrouded avenues and beaches of developing countries they don't show on TV, of which only The Shadow knows. **(16)**

Mexico: Trip 1

Taxco—Grutas de Cacahuamilpa Nat. Pk.—Mexico City—Tepoztlan

Surrounding Tepoztlan were the weathered remnants of an extinct volcano. Jagged cliff walls rose up, textured like rotten wood, but overhung with dense greenery. Winding, abrupt cobbled streets with old shade trees, the town had, with a stern church and convent. Behind, Popocatepetl and Ixtaccihuatl volcanoes were topped with snow. And the dizzy prospect from Ometochli's pyramid shrine (god of *pulque*, maguey hooch), was over a thousand tipsy feet above town.

Drinking seriously in Mexico is pre-Columbian. Many Indian tribes, such as the Tarahumara, have old-fashioned maize beer and the like for their drinking ceremonies—during which Gargantuan doses are imbibed. And unceremoniously, in or out of bars all over, spree drinking (*borrachera*), rather than laying off after one's limit, is more the norm. It being less a private vice, as in the north, than a long-established custom.

Mexico City—Puebla

A pack of schoolboys on a Puebla side street ran circles about a youthful *señorita*, yelping and hooting in teasing tones. Mean fun. Not being their babysitter, she wanted to be rid of them, but they kept after her. Was something the matter with her reputation? Mexico was feeling a few degrees more foreign.

Cholula—Tonantzintla—Acatepec

Two fantastic churches within a short walk. One with a tangled, riotously *churrigueresque* stucco interior of flying angels, tropical fruit, flowers, birds, devils, and a few saints—all in vivid, contrasting colors or gilded. The other with a brilliant façade of glazed tile: blue, yellow, and green. Much like tiled Mid-eastern mosques and tombs that Zeke saw later on. Mexico's answer to European rococo and Islamic ornamentation.

Cofre de Perote Nat. Pk.
Zeke startled awake at a bugle call near his tent. In a hurry to pitch at dusk the day before, he'd camped in short brush not far from some kind of fort, presumed to be an uninhabited relic. It was the derelict brother of the Alamo, according to its façade. But now came troops of uniformed troopers trooping outward in formation, on course for his position! Apparently without sighting him yet, though. Anxious moments . . . Would he be thrown in a brig or a dungeon?

Hup! Hup! Hup! Then, suddenly, all trooper eyes and bodies turned in unison, right-face, and away they marched that way. The army can't be wrong: dull green and tan are the best colors for a tent. Nevertheless, it was the second-rudest awakening of his camping career to date! (Only worse was that time the peacock shrieked in his ear as he slept in Hampstead Heath Park, London. Opening his eyes in terror, he could not urgently make sense of his glossy orange moped helmet lying a couple feet away, which then suddenly flared as a towering bird flapped from behind it.)

The park's volcanic summit brought into view below a corner of the Mexican Plateau. Which resembled the steep-sided giant step or butte on file upstairs as his elementary idea of how a plateau should look. A battlement of lava

Mexico: Trip 1

above tropical lands, it rose. Ranges of sharp peaks spread away below in a dim, overlapping series. Raggedy fringe of the central highlands, declining into Oaxaca State and the Gulf coast.

A natural boundary it was. Beginning to feel too much the conspicuous gringo, Zeke was latently eager to bug out. But it wasn't only that. Sleeping out three months while tramping a Third World nation was at least as uncomfortable as domestic camping had been. He was still new at it.

On some mornings he awoke, it troubled him:

> Why put up with it any longer? Once out of my tent, there awaits heat, cold, insects, dirt, wet, animal threat, or men in uniforms. Disturbances and problems which it wastes my strength to address, in one way or another, almost constantly. I do so in order to keep them from causing various levels of strain. They sap mental energy, too. It's difficult to concentrate while enduring the cold or the heat. Besides which, I get hungry for both warm food and other indoor comforts while camping and walking.
>
> Should I head for town? Not so fast! More aversive stimulation awaits in the usual world of strangers than on secluded trails. To contend with or dodge in town are an oversupply of persons unknown, many of them maybe wickeder than me. Plus: menacing machines, loud noises, air pollution, contagious disease, and a scarcity of free or dignified spots to sit or lie down for a rest, or to urinate, or to pick

Mexico: Trip 1

my nose, etc. Onlookers, always onlookers. Then, the added anxiety to make it on time.

There is constant sensory, intellectual, and emotional overload in cities. Where much energy I lose in ignoring unwanted rackets or sights—either by remaining non-responsive or reacting to such intrusions. Likewise, by rejecting or misguidedly reacting to other kinds of sensation that interfere with whatever it is I'm trying to do. If packing enough food, the woods and fields are easier to put up with, even enjoy. Although, perhaps, not indefinitely.

Then, by and by, as if on a busy street, *"Natural boundary!"* bumped into *"Save the rest for a later Central American trip."* And these two notions clung in a magnetic cathexis.

Mexico City—Chihuahua—Nogales

Now heading for home, thrifty Zeke purchased a second-class train ticket. First-class, in any case, was sold-out. All aboard! Tight standing-room-only, then darkness fell.

Both his legs and skull numbed after long train vibration through his soles. Partly to restore circulation, as he half-sleepwalked or squeeze-walked the next car, he saw a boy abed in its authentic baggage rack of rope netting. Monkey see, monkey do. Zeke racked out. Before shuteye in his swaying hammock, though, a mature woman below gave what he took as a smile of approval. What's more, it seemed unlikely that any conductor would give muscling his way through the coach a try anytime soon. **(17)**

Mexico: Trip 1

The moderately packed car at sunup felt less claustrophobic. Some had detrained. As well, he got the impression that Mexicans are quite tolerant of open eccentricities. And so, liking those yet on board for that, he forgave their crowdedness. Zeke was later to discover that in quite a few folk societies, tolerating the revealed doings of oddballs or aliens was less an issue and more a settled frame of mind. Expecting it of them, they overlooked strangers behaving strangely. In addition, in Mexico, more craziness was tolerable in minor males—period.

Early on, that republic had the side effect of soothing Zeke's over-tenderness to public disapproval. Throughout his youth, it was a rougher battle to defend his ego. Defend mostly against what fell out of his own overactive fancy, but now and again against the real thing: impudence and ridicule. They seemed more in the air up north. Mexico gave more the feeling of "anything goes."

In those days, in the north, self-reproach quickened after his pride had been prickled by overmuch public exposure and frustration. It might while making for home after some three or four months of outdoor continuance. Thorns in his hindsight, not his pants. Regrets over low points in maintaining his bearing. Travel fatigue made them worse. Off and on, his reviews of things gone by might grow congratulatory, but most were of another sort. Would he ever swell into a man of the world who knew how to conduct himself?

Much of the gloom in his younger days came from mental reruns of yesterday. He had less concern over his tomorrows. Fewer long-term anxieties weighed upon him. When one did come along, he told his mind to ignore it. Its imagery might never come about. His past had. So much so that much of the time, it made his present almost nothing. And the bossing voice nagging about his recent past, he realized, even down to the same trite phrases, was his father's.

With no specific regret available for self-punishment, Zeke now and then went in for rehearsing make-believe arguments with Daddy, or went in for memories of real ones. Dialogues containing Dad's passionate exhortations on how to alter some expensive, perilous, or nonconforming bent. With these massively refuted by Zeke's nonchalant replies. For years, it was one of his most persistent thinking habits: arguing away his father's influence. Which he did predominantly in imagination, being a mouse. While his father turned out to be an above-average guinea pig, more adept at doing anger. Thus, Zeke often practiced his nonchalance. One thing he had in common with his father, though: he was extremely sensitive to oral disapproval.

"Why not go to parks around here—why way out in California or someplace?" Dad asked. "Doesn't all woods look pretty much the same?" Or on a latter-day visit, and him an elderly man, after Zeke lowered the thermostat a bit in his sweltering house came the commonplace observation: "You think only of yourself!" Scolding Zeke was his dominant outlet for solemn anger till the day he died. Which resulted in childhood feelings of guilt and shame, later modulating into an ambivalent mix of liking and annoyance for its source.

His father was an intelligent man, though hardly an intellectual. He had an intense specialized interest. Growing

Mexico: Trip 1

up during the Depression gave a strong practical bent to his thinking. He taught business courses at a college and, before he passed on, at age 90, was worth through wise investments over two million. Until near his end, well after retirement, he kept his wealth secret, and continued with his family to live middle-class mostly in the same small town as his parents. Only his stockbroker, with perhaps some of his faculty friends and students, learned sooner that his achievements surpassed competent fatherhood.

Explaining and justifying himself to interior paternal utterances typically kept Zeke entangled in mildly angry thoughts. Even into late middle age, he still had the same justification-to-father daydreams. Out of youth, their tone became prouder, though. More often like bragging than defensive argument. "What a healthy, beautiful day's walk I'm on this morning. A type of happiness that you scarcely tasted." He didn't get over thinking frequently of Dad until after he passed away. As if his childhood experience of him had left behind a sort of low-grade, chronic trauma.

Turning him into your angry young man and social critic? Well, it's true, Zeke's angry daydreams were not only regarding his parent, but also society at large. But rarely did he press how he felt into hard-and-fast political opinions, let alone actions. Rather, his expansive, lasting teenage alienation and idealism had him hunting perfect regions of natural or artificial charm to get away from it all. He didn't often try and change society. Too reserved for that and—damn right—no good at anger.

The underlying motive for his international drifting may have been to lose his sad remembrances enough for freer intake of the here-and-now. Further, to run up against newer obstacles far afield that might then, someway, give him room to pass. His reward for giving enough mindfulness to the present juncture. A vital component of travel's appeal is how well it may fend off intruding daydreams—or at least the old, boring ones.

In other words, as a past-tense kind of guy, it was Zeke's nasty instinct to find the past more intriguing than the here-and-now or the future. So he'd try to elude his displeasing or stale memory nemesis by topping off his mind with unusual current happenstance. Dimly, he wished for that. But in place of it, forgetting to seize the present moment, most of the time he tossed about inside his dream spaces. Could be, too, he was burdened with an extra fierce compulsion to root through his past for future benefit. Whatever it came from, deciding that some category of mental functioning was counterproductive did not make it go away for long.

Forget all that, now, and flash back to his night ride on the train. In the wee-wee hours, squeezing his retreat from the filthy, stinking john, Zeke was re-passing three men leaning by an open door, upon a rattletybang car coupling. Whom those near in adjoining cars were giving plenty of room—roaring drunk, as they were. One raised high the fifth of tequila his amigo handed over, to see how much was left—not much. A hasty cry! Zeke looked again just as the tippler stumbled above the stairwell, lost his balance, one arm flailing, and fell backwards into darkness. His dropped bottle then hitting the lowermost tread, shattering, and pale brown liquid splashing upward. All slow motion in Zeke's eye memory, it remained.

Mexico: Trip 1

In the moonlight, it didn't seem the train was going at a rapid clip. He may have found his feet again after his backward flop. Maybe okay, if he came down more on grit or brush than rock. It was lightless semi-desert, though, likely devoid of help or drinks. The emergency-stop cord! If extant, somewhere among the dense throng, no one yanked it. Next morning, what he'd seen weighed in as nothing worse than sort of a nightmare. There, swinging slightly in his rope baggage rack. Yet the lingering visual memory of a man grabbing with his free hand and missing as he went down from then on became Zeke's ultimate image for how not to misbehave on a train.

Trip 2
(February–March 1995)

Tijuana—Veracruz

With the favorable dollar-to-peso exchange rate, Zeke's plane ticket to Veracruz from barely south of the border cost much less than it would have from California. Landing soon before sundown, he pitched tent in overtopping weed near the airport.

Mosquitoes got in all night through a forgotten hole in his zippered nylon netting, though. Their flight hums went undetected as he slept with earplugs through the jet roar. Hence, they made the best of it and presumed upon him. After sweating awake into a hot, humid brightening of morn, buying anti-malaria pills became an urgent concern, up there with finding a hotel.

The hotel was much harder to come by. He went all over town searching for a room and no luck. It was Mardi Gras—his first and last. One hotel receptionist said try again after a while, so Zeke plunked his luggage there, behind the counter. When he tried back, though, nothing. Many homeowners were renting spare rooms. They referred him onward, one to the next, but still no room.

A multi-lingual German came over as Zeke reposed in a plaza. Soon into their talk, he offered to assist finding and then split the cost of a room somewhere or other.

"Sure, but do you know of any?"

"Maybe. A vacant, out-of-the-way double."

He led Zeke there. It was an ill-lit garage with mattresses and carpet.

"Overpriced, but what choice do we have?" Gunter argued.

But then, Zeke was in for a jolt. When, after paying his half of the rent, "I can't afford it!" his friendly helper exclaimed. And ducked out.

Less surprisingly, the guest cottage owner not only refused Zeke a refund but forcefully served notice: "Pay the rest or out *you* go, too."

Was he the real Señor Rat or a middle-aged guinea pig with fair acting talent? In all, it cost him about like a stateside motel—was unaffordable. Although, as a bonus, a new petty travel con was revealed. Odd how much like San Blas, near the beginning of his first Mexican trip, this one was starting off. Here was another unreliable roommate. **(18)**

Xalapa—Coatepec

Some of Mexico's light-skinned body politic, Spanish holdovers, were language-patriots, like French Canadians. They worried North American culture was insidiously replacing Spanish/Mexican culture through the expansion of its language. Why, more than once, Zeke met smiling reluctance to speak English to he who freely admitted, in a thick accent, to being out of his lingual element. "No hay espanol!" Reluctance, that is, after letting about one sentence of their own English slip out—an irresistible display of academic superiority.

In spite of which, their good natures would sometimes overcome their cultural principles if Zeke, enthusiastically, made enough "Se"-s and arm signals to demonstrate he was sparing no effort to speak in Spanish, even though he couldn't. They could then easily see that his ignorance of their mother tongue was neither from distaste nor utter indifference to things Spanish (such as themselves). Nonetheless, once a teacher with earnest expression, right away, did present sufficient English to voice his concern that the new Free Trade agreement with the U.S. would further erode Spanish-language influence.

Xico—Cascada de Texolo Park

On the trail beyond Texolo cascades were the following: elephant ear lianas spreading over canyon walls; varieties of epiphytes and creepers; green-black clumps resembling mistletoe on tall trees; Spanish moss; red and yellow orchids; pink, red, and yellow wildflowers underneath; overarching tree ferns and ground ferns, too; fluttery, tiny yellow-breasted *bananaquits* in small flocks, and their finely woven nests; hummingbirds with green necks; bougainvillea on the rampage, with other flowering bushes; patches of jungle.

There were 20-ft. banana palms with long, tattered foliage and 10-ft. coffee bushes along the cobblestones to trailhead. Horses packing either bunches of green bananas longer than his arm or heaps of firewood passed, led by Mexican cowboys in white hats.

Tlaxcala—Cacaxtla ruins—San Martin—Mexico City—Amecameca—<u>Ixta-Popo Nat. Pk.</u>

Zeke shared a taxi from Amecameca up to Popo's pooh-and-trash-littered parking lot. With a long-hair from New Mexico, a kindred spirit named Ben. Since the hotel clerk had come to his door with Ben the evening before, and asked something in Spanish. "Would you allow Ben to use the unoccupied bed in your (tiny) room?" Zeke misunderstood him to say. He refused with notable irritation. Then Ben clarified in English that he, through the clerk, was only hunting for someone to go fifty-fifty on a cab up to the volcanoes next day, not for a bed.

"Why do almost all Americans met in Mexico speak the language, and I can't?" wondered Zeke. "Me no better than monoglot here." Was it essentially due to his introversion and lack of zeal for dialogue in any tongue? Studying a backup language or two at school always felt as excessive as taking out cards at far-city libraries when the local one had superfluous worthy print for a lifetime of reading.

His prime alibi, though, was his flimsy ability to learn by heart unfamiliar systems of speech. Reading in class from a German textbook, his pronunciation was near perfect, said the prof. Only when it came to recalling to what those tongue-twisting auditory phenomena referred did he fail. As if his left brain was so loaded with English that only his right had enough bytes left over to register foreign words as a sort

Mexico: Trip 2

of musical notation. (Besides outlandish lingo, spare room in Zeke's half-wittedness was lacking for either important dates or any other numerals.) "Is there a subconscious decision at some stage of growing up to habitually ignore specific types of data?" a determined believer in choice might inquire.

From where he camped, Zeke saw high, fluffy hassocks glittering yellow and tan, radiant, having the appearance of mown hay faraway. With a sparse evergreen forest yonder, below the two volcanoes' serrated rock, dark brown to the white snowline. Fleecy cloud parades crossed the volcano crowns. Then, before dusk, their snow went out of focus and acquired pastel hues of rose and lilac. At twilight, a skunk came by. After which were coyotes' howls and the muffled helloing of an owl.

At daybreak, rounded Popocatepetl peaked over the saddle, like the moon crashed to earth. Too close, huge, surreal; blue-gray and white it glittered, while clumpy pine boughs sparkled like green tinsel. Then, after a while, the sun higher, ultra otherness dividing light and the black shadow of Ixtaccihuatl began. As did a glaring temperature contrast: heat in the sun, freezing in the shadow, as the breeze blew icy cold.

Ben showed up in forenoon as Zeke was folding his tent; asked where he was going, and was going his way. Invited, Zeke felt obliged to keep him company aways more. Their chatter from the taxi resumed on the trail to Ixtaccihuatl. (Popocatepetl off and on was fuming sulfurous gas and clouds of ash into the air: trail closed. Its earthshaking eruption ultimately occurred Dec. 18, 2000.)

Mexico: Trip 2

Up the trail, high-reaching bushes were plumed with man-sized yellow flowers. Furthermore, there were: flame-red, purple, and white wildflowers; tall thistles with fuchsia tufts; yellowish-green mistletoe blobs in the pines on canyon sides; golden butterflies, brown-yellow-blue-speckled butterflies, large yellow butterflies; petite red birds with black tails and heads; needles of old lava protruding above choppy, mile-long cliffs, like the lower jaws and fangs of dreadful beasts.

Above all that a piece, the rocky way up front mounted too breakneck for Zeke's liking. He'd feel that way when a route got so precarious as to require scrambling to pursue it up out of sight and who knows how much farther. Then, slippery crushed snow underfoot began. "Damn! I forgot to pack my crampons, ice ax, and technical climbing gear again!" By which Zeke chickened out, and they went their separate ways, his being cautiously down.

It came to him that one benefit of going alone is saving face in the face of menacing topographies. Solitary, one can shrug off adventure exactly where a talus slope you've been side-footing goes vertical enough to be worrisome. One is under no peer pressure, then, to act guinea pig. To push onward a bit farther to impress guys like Ben. On the other hand, if you're apt to fall anyway, it's safer to have an audience.

No trail markers, no signposts, no map—only a single-paragraph guidebook description of the central hiking trail. Whence, Zeke proceeded to make what should have been "an easy 5–6 hour walk" into a dodgy, grueling 3-day full-scale descent. Some wicked psychiatrist might say he was using recklessness to punish himself for cowardice. Putting himself

Mexico: Trip 2

in a worse fix than likely would have come had he strung along with Ben. By then in his animate existence, though, Zeke had pretty much come to terms with his unmanliness. (Part-time even seeing wisdom in it.) Then, was what came next brainless, pure and simple? Not entirely: it was more like his brain was too distracted on the way up, talking to Ben, to remember much of where they'd come. Compelled to hold up his end of the conversation, his attention to what trail turnoffs they took faltered.

He kept to a well-worn cow path rather than follow out a severely overgrown trail. That must have been where he first went amiss. It tended the right way, though. Then, striding farther down slope through deep grass, finessing the cow pies, was all too easy. It was only partway to the bottom of a plunging, loose-dirt gully below a small waterfall that he realized his mistake. Then, touch and go out of nature's cow-trap as regaining elevation wore him out. And so Zeke camped on an attractive site when it met his eye, feeling it was one mentioned in the guidebook. Beyond, a clear trail ascended a canyon wall on the far side of a brook's low burbling. (Oddly referred to as "river" in the text.)

Anyway, next morning he took that trail about a mile, to where it abruptly dead-ended at a precipice. With a few cow bones laid before the brink as a tip-off for cows and others. Great view, though, for the living. So he backtracked, searching for another pathway to salvation, and there it was. But, it wasn't. Yet again, Zeke had chosen to straggle after deviant, untoward cows. That was obvious once he got near timberline. But the untracked forest cover then somehow made

Mexico: Trip 2

him optimistic, so he wasn't minded to turn back. Too stupid with exhaustion, additionally, to even think of thinking it over. From which, from there he went on just the same after having, with binoculars, spied way below a path or road. Onward cross-country for miles down a steep volcano, he toddled.

Going down, there were both ravines ending in cliffs and projecting lava outcrops also ending in drop-offs: two kinds of terrain to shun. While in a few situations, he had to lower his pack on a rope through thickets of spruce sapling, feeling out his footing on branches and precipitous, slippery slopes. Thorn bushes also attacked his peace of mind farther down. Eventually, a sawed stump came to Zeke's attention and a faint path. Then, beyond a maze of cow and woodchopper bypaths and crooked ways lay a trail through a scrubby gulch marked with plastic trash. "Civilization!" Dull-headed and rubber-legged with fatigue, Zeke stumbled onto the logging road at canyon bottom and soon slept. **(19)(20)**

He had hiked decades enough by then to know that every so often he made largish blunders at it. Sure, his written instructions to himself did *some* good. Howsoever, he was still really bad at making out new intersecting trails, for instance. He'd be out and walking, as in the above, and might tramp right on by what he wanted twice, forth and back, without seeing where it went off. Even when, due to his map, he'd been looking for it. Or, he might go wandering on little off-paths to nowhere.

Much of that sort of thing arose from eating THC. Which is liable to shift observation more onto the landscape or else into daydreams, away from anything so left-brained as trail-noticing. (Only of directional advantage in an area

Mexico: Trip 2

of faint, ill-defined trails, where it may temporarily lend the aid of a lingering eye in seeking one out.) Other occasional causes for his flawed path-finding included bursts of self-consciousness after coming upon people hanging about trail junctions. As did abruptly coming upon either beauty or a big eyesore—bursts of aesthetic consciousness. Whether a grand vista near a trail blaze attracted, or a stinky park outhouse near one deflected, either could jiggle his attentiveness just enough to miss his turnoff.

Zeke began conceding to himself early in his progress that he had no special talent for riding public conveyances. Yet it was not until soon after his 58th birthday that he was able to admit that he possessed little more for walking. Poor sense of distance and poor sense of direction he had, for starters. Maybe slightly above average at reading a map was all. Sheer persistence was his primary strength—the explanation for which might also partially involve THC, which often let him forget how tired or bored he might otherwise be.

Why did it take him so much longer to admit being a so-so hiker than being a so-so all-around traveler? Maybe it felt safer attaching vanity to shining at something pursued more in private; where few saw his screw-ups.

On his way out of there next morn, more misery befell. A sizable pack of yapping, snarling dogs came at him from a far bend. All together they looked and sounded monstrous. Wig-wagging his staff before their noses failed to discourage them much. They bobbed at bay in a tight circle. Some were inching closer.

Mexico: Trip 2

His pepper spray! He'd shoot a dense fog above them, causing their retreat as it wafted down to their snouts. Zeke expected no less of his high-pressure weapon, but *Psssst!* A faint hiss, barely audible, as a few drops of the irritating biochemical flew out only a few inches, then dripped onto the underbrush and his boots (size 11). What a spot to run out of gas! A minute later, though, at the bend, he glimpsed their master coming. A *campestro* on horseback leading two loaded pack horses. But Zeke mostly had to keep his eyes on the dogs.

Looking up again, he saw with half an eye the former rider on his knees roadside, rubbing his skull and chest. Apparently, he had fallen off his *cayuse* in trying to dismount and rush forward to call off his hounds. Or as it reared in fright? Zeke's close attention had been on the pack, which just then ran back to their fallen boss. Who found his legs and came forward. A big, stocky dude, who was apt to be sore. Zeke shed his pack and waited, wishing he knew enough Spanish for a magnificent apology.

Lucky for Zeke, his unintentional victim was a guinea pig—barely. He tied his horses and then came on past Zeke slow-foot to set them a good example. But, he looked the gringo over and muttered going by—within the bounds of possibility, an insult. Then in returning, he brought up and plopped down a heavy mitt on Zeke's shoulder. To see whether he'd flinch, squirm away, and throw the first punch, perhaps. Else to further reassure his furry friends up the way.

Zeke stood pat and met his gaze. After which, and a query as to his language, the *hombre* clutched his side and mimed agony. To indicate he might have cracked a rib. Next and last, he gestured that old vicious dog owners' refrain: "They never (before) have bitten anyone." Thereupon, Zeke put in some sympathetic, apologetic murmuring from beneath his eye contact, and they parted.

Tlalmanalco
Another day, another dog. In a small semi-Spanish-colonial town below the volcanoes, near where he came out, it was. There, a green car sped along the main street and struck a long-legged part-greyhound mongrel. Zeke heard the clunk, heard the squeal, and turned to see it limping away with a foreleg injury. No screech of tires either before or after impact. Why there were always scads of dead dogs along highways in provincial Mexico. Few others braked for them, either.

Those feisty back-road dogs seen yesterday, like Zeke then, were fortunate. Strays in towns looked harassed, half-starved, and unhealthy. Then there were the watchdogs short-chained to flat roofs of concrete bungalows. Which retaliated against their uncomfortable bondage by suddenly growling or barking close to the startled ears of a passerby.

Mexico City—Pachuca—Chico Nat.Pk.
Zeke got off at the mega-humongous Mexico City bus terminal again. Where a muscle man sitting behind him, taking account of his foreignness, volunteered to guide him to the proper ticket counter and boarding platform. Insisted upon carrying his backpack there, too—a major assist. He spoke some English, having had a job in the U.S.

Mexico: Trip 2

Then, forthcoming in Pachuca was more help in time of need. Overhearing Zeke refuse a gringo-priced taxi ride from the bus, another stout fellow voluntarily drove him to the one for Chico Nat. Pk. in his VW, even getting out to make clear where to wait. As kind as his big-city cousin, he was, but Zeke had to ask himself: "Am I appearing more and more friendless and needy as my journey wears on?"

The upbeat guinea pig of Pachuca made a memorable comment during their short walk-and-talk. To paraphrase: "While in the U.S., the absence of crowds on the street made me feel lonely and alien. That was one reason I returned to Mexico to live." How strange this sounded to Zeke, who so disliked jam-packed depots. And populous trails, cities, planets, and so on.

He tried to conceive what feeling lonely in a neighboring state from its having too few pedestrians on the sidewalk would be like. It strained his empathy. As six days out of seven *his* preference ran to comparatively vacant territory. How it was on the Temple of the Sun before the tourist buses arrived.

But anyhow, he thought:

> Two cities, two favors! Personally, I'm so self-interested that doing favors is rare. I'm usually more apt to regard my own little convenience as worth more than a stranger's little inconvenience. They have to be in a really bad way for my conscience to kick in and me offer them aid. Why is that? Do I associate favors with authority from long experience of my father, who was extraordinarily helpful? Me resisting

him in that along with the other ways that I resist imitating him—an identity thing?

I was his kid, not transitory, though. No, there must be motives for small-scale altruism beyond family. Okay, one glimpsed in myself is a feeling of camaraderie for all hikers—for those who share my main interest in life. To generalize it more, camaraderie for those whose minds or hearts are felt to be peculiarly similar to my own. Which is indeed a feeling of special sympathy toward particular segments of humanity outside my family—those with whom I most easily identify.

Aside from that, it's difficult to say what it is about me that inspires so much helpfulness around here, in central Mexico. Is it only that I'm close to their ideal of a fellow traveler? Or more plausibly, it's taking kindly to a grouping which bohemian influence up north teaches me to scorn. Class: it's from looking middle-class in Mexico. By no means is it ethnicity, and probably not race, either. That guy at the bus terminal had tan skin. Middle-class status may carry more altruistic weight in Mexican society than it presently does where I come from.

Huauchinango (Hooch)

Here grouchy, midlife Zeke found more justification for complaint. Bad coffee again! Alhough at least the restaurant he was in had some kind of brewed rather than a jar of instant on your table. Brewed you'd expect, as Hooch sat on volcanic

Mexico: Trip 2

soil in Mexico's coffee-growing region. Still and all, a café au lait there tasted no better, possibly worse, than what answered to the name of joe at an interstate fast-food in Texas. Alas, the economics of coffee farming in the vicinity were such that restaurant patrons derived no benefit. Agribusiness, insensibility, and poverty in combination, was it?

In any event, the patrons of pharmacies in Hooch may derive the benefit of timely warning. Zeke went in for some aspirin, and a town resident about his own age volunteered to translate. A paleface Hispanic, fluent in English, who then invited him to bed at his abode, rather than a hotel. Hence, Zeke soon unpacked his filthy camping gear in the guestroom of a Mexican middle-class home.

When he first had to come out to eat, the talk swiftly veered to what the heck he was doing in "Hooch." Drunk? Lost? Zeke whipped out his topographic map of the area and modestly indicated the trail and dirt roads that he intended to walk a few days all the way (and mostly downhill) to El Tajin archaeological zone near Papantla. Of course, his host was unacquainted with any trail where the map said; most who live near trailheads, anywhere, have road-heads and so lack all awareness of trailheads. No surprise there. But then he went on to advise against all hiking off-road in those parts. The "indigenes" were "not trustworthy," he said.

Later his host's father and a neighbor on hand both implored Zeke not to risk going way out all by his lonesome thereabouts. Zeke, nevertheless, was looking forward to the excursion—the longest on his itinerary. From high on the central Mexican plateau clear down into the Gulf Coast jungle, like that great hike he did in Bolivia. And it certainly would look bad on his hiker's resume, giving up on one for lack of derring-do, coming so soon after his Izta-Popo fiasco. His precious map would go to waste, too! Just barely, he summoned up enough trepidation about meeting up with an adventure on the trail to go with heeding an old formula inspired by a dire incident while on Java—the island—hereafter to be revealed. (21)

To be more exact, though, having had a bellyful of caffeine and too little repose that day, he put off deciding absolutely until tomorrow. Aware that a pooped mind provides fertile compost for growing fear—no definite menace, such as bloodthirsty savages, need apply. Fatigue aggravated by coffee may cause free-floating foreboding; his worry continuing to diesel in an idling mind like an overheated car motor, out of tune.

Near bedtime, with nothing much shaking, Zeke yet felt, now and then, inclined to worry about . . . just about anything. A mood plausibly nourished by his conscientious self-instructions coming thick and fast all day for eluding this or that letdown. His mind churning along in that same mode, but with no real problems to solve. Thus, if he misplaced some small belonging in his room or tent, an overwhelming certitude that it was gone for good reached crescendo. Stolen! Lost! Or then, with no missing pen or sock to annoy, there was scope for apprehension about, any day now, encountering some unknown, horrible fate. Obviously, Zeke's finer decisions were made after a good sleep—at his rested, foolhardy best. Therewith, in this instance, he upheld his prescriptive one from last evening.

Mexico: Trip 2

El Tajin ruins

Next stop, El Tajin pyramid. Hope it isn't aswarm with tourists, like the last one, was his main thought on the bus there. *Swarming!*

It worked at the last pyramid, so why not the same here in this intriguing jungle habitat? Camp near the scene for a jump on the tourists. Therefore, at twilight, as a cacophony of bird cries rang over the canopy, he did. Through another jaguar-free night. And soon after sunrise, he hid his pack near the campsite. Which had no view of the pyramid, though was level and soft enough, with mosquitoes not so troublesome, but quite a few ants. Only on the exterior of his tent's mended netting, though.

One of the park guards smiled and asked agreeably, "Camping?" As Zeke burst from the bush soon after sunrise on the far side of the ruins from the car park. He looked patently Indian and trustworthy. (The guard, not Zeke.)

The highest, most fantastic pyramid of the group was not unlike a cubed Hindu *sikhara* temple. Levels of right-angled niches rising, it had, like the windows of a wedge-shaped, space-age office building or a honeycomb for square bees. Dig: pyramids old as time made by square bees, or maybe giant ants . . .

Green jungle hills enclosed the pyramids: samples of imposing old stonework blotched brown and white. With languid orange butterflies, yellow ones, giant blue ones, yellow and black ones, floating by ponderous geometric shapes. Droopy vines with orange blossoms were in the dense tropical hardwoods, from which came elaborate bird calls, hummingbirds,

and whirring-wing brown doves. High above circled birds of prey.
Zeke's gear was right where he left it, a short way into the forest fringe. All in order— until he got closer. Suddenly, it went all blurry! The surface of his backpack swarmed. Gingerly unzipping the flap for a quick look inside, army ants dashed up his forearms, too. Alien! Disgusting! The deepest recesses of his pack—food, sleeping bag, clothes—minutely in motion. Swarming! (22)

Papantla—Pachuca—<u>Penas Cargadas Park</u>
Zeke began crawling over the map in the direction of San Miguel de Allende, his next stopover. First, though, he had to retrieve surplus stuff from a Pachuca hotel storage left behind for his round trip to the coastal plain pyramid. That twilight he camped near town and next day walked to a place which had only tentatively (parenthetically) rated a visit on his itinerary. It came up a winner!
There were giant gray obelisks rearing aloft from the base of a mount. The highest had a chunky headpiece on a thinner neck, balanced on a hefty torso. It looked like an exalted extraterrestrial, hip-deep in evergreens by a yellow meadow. But, up close, the other-worldly invader resolved itself into a rock garden for tiny cabbage-like cactus, for vine cactus with yellow flowers, and for other pygmy kinds of sandy-soil plant on moss. These were the terrestrial germs that would ultimately cause the alien's downfall—unless it was the other way round, and they were huge Martian parasites, resembling miniature cacti, soon to wipe out man.

In the meantime, though, there was peace and tranquility. Under the giant in the sunshiny meadow, with its brook, were boys herding sheep and a man with his donkey, chopping firewood: mesquite, acacia, pine.

Pachuca—Mexico City—<u>San Miguel de Allende</u>

On a hill, one- or two-story row houses of plastered brick, adobe, or stone: white, pink, pastel blue, or green. Often having broad, block-long, horizontal bands of brown or gray, painted head-high, above narrow cobble walkways. A refined artistic version of a steep hillside barrio in Pachuca that, in turn, resembled the yet more authentic Indian pueblos of the U.S. southwest.

The hillside barrio baked in the midday sun. But there in San Miguel, the tight cobbled, flagged, or dirt streets remained shady with lower temperatures all day. It featured wrought-iron balconies; courtyards with antique, stagnant fountains and imprisoned tropical flora, stone lintels and wooden doors, both carved; architectural cartouche; "Bar Salons" with swinging cowboy doors; massive vines luxuriating over high walls into cobbled alleys; red bougainvillea; white herons roosting on park treetops; rows of trim, one-story topiary hedges, their boughs low to the wind, same height as the housing. Also about were violet flowering jacara trees.

Zeke roamed to and fro among its streets. Morning sun glistened off the flagstones, golden metallic, cobbled riffles of light. Fantastical colors shone an hour before sunset. A town of disheveled grace, not self-consciously neat. Only cars, telephone wires, and TV antennae anchored it in modern times, and even so it drifted.

Guanajuato

The Museum of the Mummies (!!!) was packed. Inside hung the odor of the grave, sanctity, or armpits. Zeke smelled something bad! Anyhow, here was a retrospective show of dead ancestors, their corpses naturally preserved by minerals in the soil and arid atmosphere, grotesque forms with twisted features. Grubbed up to make legroom in the graveyard, they were, for other bodies; cadavers bent upon post-mortem stardom.

Along highways all over, sprouting up from litter, rose many short crosses. These being homemade memorial markers on-the-spot of fatal automobile accidents. Did bigger crosses on Mexican peaks mark airplane crashes? Zeke began to wonder. Anyway, crosses along roads to mark the sites of violent deaths (murders before cars) was an old Spanish custom that had persisted remarkably well, and been elaborated. Beyond a shadow of doubt, he was among a people for whom death packed a lively interest—even a morbid one.

On newsstands, thick as flies on rotting flesh, were special tabloids devoted to photos of car-crash and murder victims. Graphic butcher-shop details, unlike the stylized violent deaths of typical Hollywood photography. Then also, hallowed by tradition, were church canvases illustrating every variety of bloody wound that Christ or some holy martyr, in a sadistic artist's bible vision, might possibly have suffered. Bullfights caught on in Mexico as a remnant of the Spanish heritage, too. While on the yearly Day of the Dead, the Indian folkway of eating skull-shaped cakes and candies went down. According to U.N. data, Mexico annually vies with Columbia, El Salvador, and Honduras for world's most homicides per capita. What to make of such facts? "Conquistador Pirates Vs. Aztec Cannibals," another blockbuster action film.

On the outskirts of the same town, and not far enough from a busy highway, was <u>Hacienda San Gabriel de Barrera</u>: a sprawling, yellow, Spanish colonial mansion and formal garden. A paradise park where once sat the silver-processing facility responsible for its 17th-century owner's wealth. An old-time model for green industry displaying temperate through tropical trees, vines, shrubs, and flowers. Creepers and climbers dangled from lattices and covered a brick-vaulted rock arcade. A crafted stone fountain spouted at the sun.

In the low hacienda, cool without air-conditioning, were brown tile floors surrounding a courtyard. Interiors were furnished with inhospitable carved furniture, though. Hadn't the cushion been invented? As if that weren't uncomfortable enough, a low, exposed ceiling beam for head-knocking divided the somber main room. On whose wall a bizarre emblematic portrait showed blood and milk squirting from Jesus and Mary, respectively, into the mouth of a kneeling saint (or lord of the manor?).

To the medieval mind, with earthly life no more than a brief, squalid interlude, indoor furnishings could be mostly overlooked. Spanish Catholicism emphasized asceticism. So, here, did the harsh interior décor uphold a Gnostic disdain for evil worldliness, the hacienda's splendid garden standing either for the seductiveness of naturalism or superiority of Heaven?

Zeke stayed at an inn reminiscent of a hacienda in structure. All floors opened on a central, tiled courtyard. Such hotels, popular in Mexico, were cooler, but noise from below bounced upward, as through an elevator shaft or megaphone. And every real Mexican hotel short of posh came equipped with one or more insistent sources of loud noise. Volkswagens idled long in their courtyards—mini parking garages by night—or a watchdog barked constantly, or a radio resounded: brand-spanking-new asceticism.

There in Guanajuato, where mummies made their home, arose noise enough to wake the dead. The TV in the lobby blasted trains of thought off their rails and out of Zeke's mind. Way in second-floor-rear, with the door closed and earplugs, the din continued. Zeke could not find "Please turn it down!" in his Spanish phrasebook—problem 1. Nor, when he reached the lobby and desk, with his accent, could he have bellowed forte enough to be understood—problem 2. And were he understood, that would expose his gringoish sensitivity, and might be ignored, he felt—problem 3.

Down in the lobby, Zeke sat facing the idiot box awaiting an opportune moment. Then, into the last commercial but one, he slunk over and turned the thing down. But the unsleeping desk guy kept it under ceaseless observation. Presto, he clicked it back up again with his remote, without audible comment. Gracious in defeat, Zeke left the field and slouched upstairs.

As for the winner below, he magnanimously turned his volume a mite lower after Zeke got in bed again.

Thanks to earplugs, he slept. But soon after midnight, he wakened to motorcycle revving and then a surge in TV volume. A new shift? Arrival of the owner? To awake him past a short interval as a practical joke? After that the TV kept on full blast until about 3 a.m. The desk clerk's bedtime?

At dawn came a church bell's tinny clangor. The Mexican signal that once again the powers of darkness have abated, making the streets safe for sleepers to get up and emerge. More wake-up calls followed: a barking mutt, a PA system from farther downtown, and then a merry uproar in the hall—more than likely, staff arriving.

After a few weeks in Mexican hotels, it seemed to Zeke that numbness to auditory stimuli did not go far enough as an explanation for all the racket. Neither did machismo. Rather, here was a breed, not trying to prove anything by it, which had a distinct partiality for background noise, of no matter what sort—seemingly, more for safety or diligence on the job than pleasure. Not only pricier restaurants and hotels, but also deluxe buses often depended upon TVs or radios almost as loud as a California leaf blower to make certain those in charge stayed alert.

Leon—Ciudad Juarez

When earplugs are no longer enough, it comes time to holler "Adios!" at old Mexico. Leon airport, for all its jet rumble, lay in reach as the swiftest way out. But he should have known that flights to all northern Mexican cities must be reserved days beforehand. He was attempting long-distance travel on the wrong bearing again: north. She advised Zeke to enter his name on the airport wait-list. But after spending a tidy cab fare to the terminal, and most of an afternoon, queuing for a seat that never materialized, then repeating the same next morning, Zeke grudgingly decided, as a last recourse, to exit overland. **(23)**

Trip 3

(January-March 2002)

Zeke felt like another Mexican vacation—don't ask why. This time, down Baja, he drove. It was a less-populous division of the country, and many of the desert whereabouts he wanted could not be attained via bus. Add to this that he was challenged by reports that Baja had the world's worst roads. Might driving, short of drag racing, at last turn as exciting as automobile advertising promised—more like a sport?

For enough concentration and suspense, driving stood in need of more road hazard: so all Zeke's experience behind the wheel that far indicated. The everyday jeopardy of crashing on overfull California highways was no longer enough to hold his interest. He was nearly asleep at the wheel. But steering so as to evade getting stranded in sand on an unpaved byway—that might do it, qualify as sport, with suitable equipment.

First off, a 4-wheel drive vehicle could be eliminated out of hand. Where would be the gamble or the achievement from competing against sandiness in one of those? Well, sir, it just so happened that Zeke already owned precisely the sort of vehicle to push the driving of a 760-mile desert peninsula almost into the category of endurance road-racing. A machine basic enough to require all his skill and daring, closer to a sailboat than a motorboat: a 15-year-old, 2-wheel drive Dodge clunker van!

Mexicali—Canon de Guadalupe

Customs formalities went amazingly fast. The immigration agent, handily standing boothless in the street, only glanced at his driver's license, grinned, and motioned him along. Zeke did not look tough enough to pose much of a threat to rough-and-tumble Mexican society, even while driving a big van.

Soon he was on a long back road to an oasis said to be *bueno* for a day hike. Toward its end, with breakneck rocky dips and hills complicated by deep sand, this road to ruin turned into the worst he'd ever been on. Worst of the worst roads—the Baja legend proven out! And probably more where this one came from.

As he went along, that back road came to be a steady font of cheerful care. Ample driving skill requisite: to steer clear of being seized by its shifty margins or its central sandbars. In fact, getting there was more exciting than his destination, which had only numerous campers beside a lazy stream with low falls. It came to mind over and over: "I've never enjoyed driving so much in my life!"

On the return, he was taken by roadside junk. The rust-colored car chassis, originally overturned on their roofs for fun, had by now rusted through and collapsed on themselves, as if squashed for scrap shipment in nature's wrecking yard.

The parched bones of motorcars that never made it. While in weathered garbage dumps or dumplets of yore, dissolving tin cans had also flattened, cropping out as big brown flakes, like autumn leaves. Northern Baja had to be where the "found objects" or "junk collage" artists of Los Angeles come for supplemental inspiration.

Tecate—Valle de Guadalupe
Zeke pulled off for the night far within a web of ranch tracks amongst an olive orchard big as all outdoors. Bare of fruit that season, so he was betting on no early-bird pickers or guards. Besides, his van was hid in a dell, down faint wheel ruts. Yet, in some way, his presence was detected.

He opened his eyes into a flashlight beam. It came through a crack in his van's cardboard window covers. BANG! BANG! BANG! Pounding on the door. At which stood two bulky *hombres*, without uniforms or credentials. Still, one said Spanish for "police," which Zeke knew. And they *did* look earnest and sober enough for the law. "No hay español!" he shouted, afraid. Once out, they only demanded in sweeping silent-film gestures that he follow them in his car. "Keystone cops in need of wardrobe," he began to think.

All the way into town, Zeke punished himself with suspense: "Am I now under arrest for trespassing?" But no: they only ordered him with more handwaving to sleep parked by the *zocolo* out front of their station. "Ah! You want me to park and snooze *here* all night?" Zeke then signaled and pidgin-Spanished simultaneously—fluent with relief, and from an urge to make nice conversational sounds while radiating cheer.

Waking time, and he was silently preparing to fade away. But the more alert-looking of the two constables, who must have been watching for him, came out, smiled, and gave a lengthy pantomime warning. Someone, if a loco gringo parked in an unsuitable spot, might: (1) smash his van's window; (2) punch him; (3) or cut his throat; (4) and rob him. Here was another urgent admonition about regional danger for a foreigner, like at Huanchinago on his last migration south. Upon this occasion, though, it came from a *mestizo*, and was about generic roadside ruffians rather than remote, indigenous countrymen. A lot of goodwill for travelers from the north existed in Mexico, and it often expressed itself as concern for their safety.

Ensenãda

Miles before town, gas fumes began wafting into the old van's interior. A full tank had gone down about twice its normal rate over the last couple days. A laconic mechanic in Las Vegas had reported his fuel pump was leaking—end of message. Such an unwelcome comment near the beginning of a long trip! So Zeke reckoned it was no more than a small chronic drip, like a runny nose—no worse than the van's ongoing oil and steering-fluid leaks. Minor, not worth repairing, he preferred to suppose. Expecting his engine or transmission to go any month now, repairing the contraption more than he had to didn't seem cost-effective.

What an idiot he'd been in ignoring a timely mechanical hint! As there, in desolation, where few mechanics spoke any English at all, he was nearly asphyxiating with the windows

Mexico: Trip 3

rolled down. With the gas stink, his fuel gauge mingled worry over running out of gas in parts unknown. Sick machinery had him in its power! **(24)**

Zeke made it into town and then to a garage recommended by the state tourism agency. After a phone call by them translated what was wrong and got a price. So, at the garage, Zeke recited the sinister phrase "bomba de gasolina," and that was all he needed. A prompt, reasonable repair, it was. (Could any denouement have been less adventurous? Some macho hero of the highway would have lit a cigar and set about fixing the sucker on his own, way out in that waste.)

Unhappily, a run to the bank was then unavoidable before leaving town. After the withdrawal, back in his van, Zeke studied a road map to find the city street or road name/number combination that would unlock his line of advance south. When, out of nowhere, a man began tapping on his right-front window, asking by circling his forefinger that he roll it down. But it chanced that very pane had been stuck closed from when he bought the thing. So an exaggerated shrug, palms up, was Zeke's answer. Twice he tapped, the guy was so insistent. Then he shifted around the van to the driver's side.

Too aggressive: wearing a San Diego University sweatshirt and toting a fat manila file in one mitt, he still fell short of looking like a student. Over-age with two red scars on one cheek, and that was only the half of it. Zeke began seeing him as a macho trying to impersonate a college boy: rat not guinea pig. Shouting extremely broken English, he claimed to recognize Zeke from somewhere. A dueling fraternity?

His map-reading felicity rudely interrupted, Zeke felt only a desire that this annoying intruder bug off. So he didn't bother opening the locked door a crack alongside him to hear better. Rather, he raised and tapped his wristwatch—one excuse. Then made another vague finger movement to indicate change of course—another excuse. For the San Diego U. alumnus had caught Zeke in a strangely obstinate mood. It showed on his ordinarily agreeable kisser—unsmiling, he was. And his wide eyes were hid behind sunglasses for the highway. So he didn't look quite as mousey as usual.

Zeke remembered his tear gas only after the curious scholar gave a dirty stare and went away. Only then did another odd thing about his unlikely old acquaintance come to mind: the guy's extremely energetic nervousness, betrayed by his mien and motions. It was a quality all the more unnatural in Mexico. But those days, many rats were strung out on speed. Its presence beneath a personality might escape notice at first.

This banking incident came early, on a suburban street of a small city, with *mucho* motor and some pedestrian traffic. Zeke had a hunch, had he let Señor Diego into his car, that he would have drawn a weapon. And the policeman's warning of a few days before rang incredibly providential.

Ensenada—Desierto Central Nat. Pk. (!!!)
Army roadblocks were every few hundred kilometers to catch smugglers.

"Any drugs or guns?"

"No."

"No guns and no woman?" smiled the guard.

"She ran off with my gun!" Zeke replied while fluttering two digits like running legs. The guard chuckled loudly and waved him on. The reward for hearing an unexpected retort to a favorite conventional gibe. As the primal male Mexican tease of another male attests that he has no female near him—with the suspicion of his having none anywhere. Which Zeke got, now and again, on both sides of the frontier. A needling of his questionable virility in taxis, in restaurants, in hotel lobbies, and so forth. "Don't cry!" was another old favorite. Teasing with what their parents taught them as a child: a family-oriented people.

The mode of wisecrack opposite tactless-aggressive is self-deprecating/self-affirming. For instance, a defensive joke after making or mentioning a personal mistake. "I may not be the sharpest tool in the shed, but I get the job done." (From an aging hippie in Mendocino County, California.) This sort of practiced quip, or Zeke's more original effort—feints at self-mockery—seldom fell on the ear south of the border. "Due to more instinctive role-playing and less introspection, they haven't as much ironic distance on themselves." That some figure of fun with a goatee determined to put wit on the couch might opine. "What's the matter with you, señor?"

> *"Laughter is the language of the Soul."* —Pablo Neruda
> *"Life is a tragedy when seen in close-up, but a comedy in long shot."* —Charlie Chaplin

"On the same general topic, visual humor is extremely popular with Mexicans." (It said in Zeke's next thought balloon.) Cartoons stalked the land! Think or talk balloons gave

Mexico: Trip 3

them air support. As did Mighty Mouse, who, flying over with his X-ray vision, would often see likenesses of all his eentsy-weentsy pals in Mexican markets or homes. They showed up on T-shirts, panties, walls, mirrors, everything underneath. While other comic-book habitués, those created by native talent, were seen in bus and laundromat waiting rooms, about as often as real-life celebrities were in photo magazines.

Trailing a string of small circles below them, more thought balloons arose from Zeke's upper extremity, and inside them were these concise paragraphs:

> Arguably, the dominant modern genre of Mexican art is the fresco. Orozco's much acclaimed, cartoonish fresco style is comparable to that of prehistoric Maya murals. These, like the Paleolithic painted rocks of central Baja, especially those near San Francisco de la Sierra, are judged as artful as the famous cave doodles at Lascaux and Altamira in Europe.
>
> It's as if a troupe of comic characters had been cooling their heels in Mexico from time immemorial. Doing their thing on the rocks, in or out of caves. The Aztecs, Maya, and other Mesoamerican empires then employed them at their sacrificial temples. Eventually, new priests from Spain showed up. Their holy theistic cartoons decorated the magic stained-glass panes of their hollow stone temples. Orozco and other late arrivals inherited and extended Mexico's petroglyph, Mesoamerican, and Christian cartoon traditions with secular themes.

Then, up the boulevard comes Donald Duck from Hollywood. Mobile, animated, driving a funky dump truck overloaded with talk and thought bubbles to help with comic-strip exploits. Was it all a strategy for reclaiming their former glory, lost when artists turned away from using toons to represent venerable ancestors, honored prey, and so on? Right out of the collective unconscious mind and into vogue popped Mickey Mouse and all his iconic colleagues—yakking, performing, advertising, drawing attention to themselves afresh, on screen and on paper.

Whereupon, here he is today, a mouse who assumed the guise of a man! Or vice versa! More like a biographer than a portrait painter, the cartoonist selects enough memorable particulars from a subject so that he or she is recognizable without other, less-telling, ones. Furthermore, though cartoonists represent with a more naturalistic grade of symbol than writers, their drawing does merge at last with language—medium for the most unforgettable depictions. (Across the street from talk balloons, ideograms live next door to pictograms.)

Portions of film animations, too, turn out to be extra retrievable from memory for some—from my very own, for example. It retains snatches of comic animation for days after their intake, as funny flashbacks. Active images of any kind may affect both attention and memory more than still ones do.

And, the same way poetry's images by their rhythms may return all at once, packing diverse feelings, so may moving cartoons come back, though usually packing only laughter. From their being closer to pictorial language, as in poetry, than other kinds of pictures are.

Virtually everyone likes to feel happy. Me again, as a prime example. I like it so much that I'll snicker, even alone, if whatnot comes into my silly head as enough excuse. To which end, via memory, I might, all of a sudden, feel inclined to whisk off to Springfield and join the Simpson family. Where reality is more obviously funny. Remembrance grabs onto those words or images with which strong feelings are bound up. Genuine laughter is a symptom of such a feeling.

And that's not all, folks! Auxiliary to their psychological significance, cartoons convey a metaphysical resonance. HAR! HAR! HAR! Seriously. Much of what makes a cartoon funny or spellbinding is the detachment it keeps from reality. It puts its audience farther away from suffering and striving than realism mostly wants. It being closer to nonspecific with its subject. In the interests of which, much physical complexity is removed from reality, and certain distortions are applied. As if highlighting it from a remote or aloof point of view from out in the heavens.

Mexico: Trip 3

What's more, seeing humanity as no grander than animated cartoons indulges them with a shade of relief from morals, frustration, and fear. Since, first off, comic stooges are normally immune to permanent injuries and death, no matter how big a Safe crashes on them. (The irony!) Don't waste your pity or worry on toons, or your censure, either. Seeing as how their laughable assaults and other sins are as far from moral concern as the doings of fairytale figures (their oral precursors). Indeed, they all occupy a domain beyond ethical standards. Better yet, everyday reality is seen as a comic rather than tragic obstruction to cartoon will. Goodbye, frustration! All in all, their version of living is short on care and brimful of vitality.

No more putting it off, kids—here comes the jubilee! Those cartoons, you know, could depict the angle of vision of a Transcendental Entity that oversees and regulates all earthly affairs. The cartoon world could model what an all-powerful alien presence, at a far remove and with undisturbed intelligence, might see as the human condition. Being One so indifferent to all the unpleasant aspects of human existence—such as physical bodies and their mortality—as to remain calm about their troubles, unmoved except—here's the thing—to laughter.

No wonder, then, cartoons have so much appeal to profoundly religious folk like the Mexicans.

Animal or human spirits as seen through timeless eyes, they be—seen impassively, as remote outward appearances. As if through a visionary union with the perception of one amoral divinity. An infinite God to whom finite sins and disasters on Earth are a source of amusement: live-and-learn mishaps with temporary consequences for piffling souls immature in love and understanding.

Comic cartoon animation may be appreciated by a broader spectrum of taste, counting children, than any other genre save popular music. Wider than arts made from either language alone or combined with realistic cinematography. All because watching animation for a while has such a positive aftereffect on mood. Realizing the laughable side of ordinary existence does that.

The thing about laughter: it mostly comes out of a short and sweet suspension of living concerns. A thing laughable is seen with utmost remoteness, beyond the social or personal horizon. Laughter turns on while feelings of sympathy or identity flicker off. A short ecstasy of liberation from the ego's striving for competence, virtue, and staying alive. Coming from a lightning-bolt awareness of bodies, counting in one's own, as no greater than other organic matter. Is hilarity a foretaste of how souls will be when split off from their bodies after death?"

Mexico: Trip 3

"Whoops! We're here," Zeke said to himself. "Desierto Central."

Unearthly *boojum* (*cirio*) trees: lengthy stems with twiggy green hair and fluffy yellow tips, bending like pretzels or upright. Then there were gangling black trees with long, smooth limbs, green pom-pom tipped, like octopuses with hand puppets. Plus: 10-ft. agave (Spanish sword) with puffy saffron blooms; low prickly pear cactus patches with lemon-yellow flowers; barrel cactus; cholla—nasty as they look; elephant trees with golden bark, peeling to reveal olive green; acacia; mesquite; ocotillo; yucca.

Going through populated regions, Zeke was bedeviled by currents of brainwave commencing: "This should be . . . That should be . . . He should be . . . She should be . . . They should be . . . I should be . . . ." Opinions transmitted by moral or aesthetic impulses. (Or as his built-in critic might say, "critical impulses," the idiot!) While in the boondocks, his reverie was more likely to begin: "This is . . ." Out there sprang an existential impulse comparable to his moral or aesthetic ones. (However far he may or may not have been from being an absurd existentialist.) The subjects of his thinking seemed often to depend on his setting.

Walking city streets, he'd have notions with a utopian slant on social topics or have introspective ones: our animal heritage, super-sanity, or something on that order. In rural solitude, such as Desierto Central, his streams of consciousness ran into metaphysics or theology. He only had to quench a thirst for psychological theorizing there when his very own ego was still parched and irritated from town or the road.

Mexico: Trip 3

Just then he was in the wilds of northern Mexico. For laughs, Zeke began thinking of God, jotted some of it down, polished it when he got home.

Cartoons depict reality in a slightly abstract manner, though less than numbers do. Which is why, in the gap between cartoons and numbers, "God" may be put to good use, like the X,Y,Z in algebra: to represent an unknown quantity or quality. In plain language, it may function as a handy word signifying the unobservable or, as of now, unknowable aspects of human being, or of what's what with the universe. A marvelous, subtle beyond or within which is not open to direct perception.

Aristotle, father of science, was of the opinion, according to Bertrand Russell, that ". . . in so far as men are rational, they partake of the divine, which is immortal. It is open to man to increase the element of the divine in his nature, and to do so is the highest virtue." This portrays reason, higher consciousness, as being a dynamism of physics or biology, like energy: some of it in all human minds, but most of it unattached.

Russell elsewhere referred to God as a "differential equation." Which may have been something like an insiders' joke for mathematicians. In as much as most differential equations defy sufficient comprehension for their solutions. And that said, figuring what's what with even the solvable ones is hard.

Mexico: Trip 3

A theory in which God figured might come to be the solution in physics to its current problem with "singularity": what you get in black holes, the beginning of the universe, and so on. Areas in space or time where, hypothetically, all scientific equations and laws turn out to be inapplicable and infinities reside. Scientific theory seems now to have hit a level of unfolding beyond which it runs into God. (Although the first theorist of physical science to clearly perceive that won't win any Nobel Prize.)

Quantum physics marks the scientific discovery that other laws may obtain for other levels of magnitude. Consequently, every bit as much as merely approximate statistical truth applies to the molecular level, far-fetched speculations about God, in words beyond testing, may be as good as it gets for describing yet smaller, sub-subatomic magnitudes. Or describing much larger magnitudes than physics currently makes out. Sizes well on their way to infinity in either direction.

Einstein, as Newton before him, casually used "God" in his verbal explanations. ("Science without religion is lame. But religion without science is blind," he said.) Many famous stars of physics put to use The Word. If it was good enough for them, then "God" may continue to serve us as a universal language catch-all term for the incalculable. And the enormous moral baggage freighted by this word in religions of long-standing may also have more worth than a mediocre standup comedian is willing to admit."

With that, Zeke decided to give God a rest.

Road: to San Jose de Magdalena

Too pretty to drive, it was. Backdrop of blue ocean and sky, reposing above rock-studded knobs luxuriant with yellow grass. A flock of doves winged out of an arroyo. On hillsides were low, bushy trees with smooth white bark, as was palo verde, mesquite, cardon, and organ pipe cacti. Mats of creeping cactus were. Buzzards were soaring. The yearning coo of doves came to ear.

Then came a wee oasis, green among rearing, reddish hills: fan palms; reeds and weeds bending with fresh breeze on a hot day; purl of a streamlet trickling over flat, smooth slabs; fleecy olive algae on the depthless water's bottom; the tranquility of a lazy stream; faint breaths of wind, at long intervals, loud-sounding in comparison, accentuating the silence. A few small birds were twittering. Isolated from the side road above, it was, by ochre, gray, and terra cotta rock bluffs. An orange dragonfly hovered over a green pool.

Roadside at a sharp curve was a cross made of two auto chrome strips, hung with a synthetic wreath, plastic red roses near. There were glass jelly jars by the memorial, too, holding bunches of real flowers, dying.

Mulege—Loreto—Puerto Escondido

Not long after another army checkpoint, a grinning drunk or maniac, driving a white pickup, wearing a white T-shirt,

Mexico: Trip 3

oncoming, spontaneously decided to play chicken with Zeke at about 50 miles per hour. His wheels swept well over the center line on collision course. Grinning like a fiend: steer and elude death! With right tires balancing along the pavement's margin, Zeke's van missed sideswiping by inches. A dodgy macho gesture of any kind, to set oneself up, is known as a *chimaeras*.

Commonplace Mexican macho antics, all in all, were more ego-threatening than life-threatening. Although often done in a more conspicuous style than seen elsewhere—more so than Italy. Stuff like insulting hand-signals at gringos in passing, or a quick clownish dance for Zeke's seated benefit by a grownup lout at the airport once, to assault his sense of propriety. But lengthy stares were preferred, as dares, to bolster boyish morale. Piercing, sustained one-note whistles when a frail-looking male walked by were also popular. (With gays?)

Zeke grew expert on the neglected topic of showy contempt emanating from adult male strangers, presumably rats. Chiefly due to the fact that, unlike him, other male mice were not so easily typed from aways off. What manner of man could put up with such insults without knocking off a bottleneck on the bar and going for them? Your basic geek: big eyes, narrow shoulders, flat chest, long neck, prone to radiate agitation by muscle tightness or automatic subordination signals. While other mice might be broad-shouldered, stocky, with swarthy complexions or beards, and menacing chins. Of more forbidding aspect, and more intent upon grooming for a conventional social role, too—such as tattooed gangster in black. It made them less-conspicuous targets.

Mexico: Trip 3

Now is a goody-good time to affirm that sympathetic, humane people do not abuse the characters of strangers through branding them with invidious labels. They rank every fellow human being as, potentially, like a brother, sister, or friend. Individual value and dignity are conferred upon them in thought and deed. Yes, surely this was Zeke's outlook upon all mice and guinea pigs, regardless of their race, creed, or gender. But now go off campus and sell it to the townie rats!

Returning to the subject of Mexicans: on average, Zeke found them civil or downright kind. Anger was less often seen than it was up north. Smart-enough ladies and gentlemen were usually soft-spoken and modulated. Conversations with outsiders were often imbued with warmth, and oodles of eye contact, too. Them being as well-mannered toward gringos as to most classes of Latino. And all this only became less true of those living in southern California, which was obviously having a bad influence.

La Paz

At the government office selling topographic maps, a restless *hombre* held himself straight behind the service desk. He mimed impatience by jittering unnaturally, but didn't come right out and complain. All he did was settle his gaze on him as Zeke leafed nervously back and forth through a guidebook, trying to lay hands on multiple road maps and hike descriptions. After which, with more dispatch than he should have tried for, Zeke chose three suspiciously costly topos and made off.

Self-consciousness while there interrupted his current of thought continually, like static. Due to someone whose manner implied that Zeke was wasting too much of his precious workday. Well, *that* one could qualify as only "critical." But any who came across as outright aggressive, sexy, god-like, incomprehensible, or stupid might put him off just the same. Zeke bottling up glimmers of annoyance with any of the above diluted his thinking. Such, however, is constantly what mice who read people via empathy must go through while trying to get things done in public.

Being ill at ease saps concentration. Where *was* his woman? But having either a familiar and trusted onlooker, or even a more neutral one than the impatient *hombre*, there that day, could also have hurt Zeke's concentration. From their making comments at inopportune moments and so forth.

Thereafter, out of town, in planning his first hike, it came to light that only about half his sought-for trail showed, way down in the corner of one map. "*Dup!*" Scanning and organizing a mix of printed description and maps, while matching them with maps of different scale, like so many things requiring close study, is better done in private. **(25)**

Zeke experienced far less stage fright while out and about in a car. That being the normal outgrowth of driving, and its greatest utility after haste—the main reason why so many were running around town in high-powered armor rather than walking or cycling. For all of that, there were some big trade-offs in using a mobile hideout and hidden vantage point. For one, there was worry over damage to their dear hunk of property—or to human bodies bouncing off it. Auto collisions happened by chance every day all over. (While getting enough exercise didn't.)

Mexico: Trip 3

Zeke drove here and there in La Paz, pursuing a cheap repair for his clown car's carburetor. A scarcity of traffic signs gave concern. Many stop signs were missing or had palm fronds over them, as did many street signs, too. Some that were pried off may have been sold for scrap, others vandalized. Some that survived were too weathered to make out. Scanning signs in Spanish as he rolled by was troublesome, but their absence at crucial corners worse.

He made some wrong turns upstream on one-way streets, and ran a few camouflaged stop signs, but actually ran up *against* nothing—near misses, no hits. In or out of town, the highway patrol and other motorists struck Zeke as astonishingly indulgent of driving eccentricities compared to up north. So that every day of rolling along the streets in La Paz, with no wreck or ticket, his feel of driving security swelled. He was on a motorist's winning streak! But as soon as the carb got fixed, he picked up his chips while still ahead and beat it.

Todos Santos

"The spiritual world is one single spirit—a light behind the bodily world and which, when any single creature comes into being, shines through it as through a window. According to the kind and size of the window, less or more light enters the world. The light itself, however, remains unchanged." —Nasafi

"Blankness is not emptiness; we may skate upon an intense radiance we do not see because we see nothing else." — John Updike

An art colony with surfing or vice versa, it was. Many of the colonists had temporary tans. English was more commonly spoken there. Near the plaza was plastered-brick native architecture, preserved from new-fashioned incongruities and most advertising. Row-house façades were textured, color-coordinated brick frames for open doorways into art galleries, picturesque and horticultured.

Most of Todos Santos' beauty was indoors and portable, though. "But why go in there instead of the surf?" a surfer asks and points. "Isn't that a beautiful wave?" "Well, my hunting indoor stimuli for aesthetic pleasure is but one motive to go after art. Another is the possible arousal of fresh ideas. And this town is good for both." From dazzling sunlight in the street, a swift transformation, out of the sun, through old, flowery doorways, into cooler depths. Which were hung with a mixture of abstract and representational canvases, sculpture, jewelry.

An insight on the relation of light, objects, representations of objects, and symbols lit his mind:

> Below the paintings are printed words and numerals, their titles and prices. A standardized symbolization which provides more widely understood messages than their artwork. Since more have enough patience to read than to contemplate visual charm or novelty. And patience is needed, since the colored canvases communicate more ambiguous plays of light than print does. Why is that? Because black letters on white are farther removed than colored works of art from being all-inclusive depictions of the sunlight spectrum on real objects.
>
> These letters on their signs, in their turn, are more ambiguous than the numerals indicating prices.

Which essentials in the language of business and science are at another yet farther remove from the ambiguity of both light and the world it reveals.

All of which suggests that the farther displaced from sunlight and the things that reflect it, the more effective artificial forms get to be for producing accepted meaning among Earthlings. What am I saying by that? Only that to human awareness, numerals are less ambiguous than words, which are less ambiguous than fairly naturalistic pictures, which in turn are less ambiguous than either nonrepresentational art or the natural world and its light.

Now, from there, admit the probability that important things presently beyond human understanding do exist. Then conceive this: to see either the sun or God only through a glass, darkly, may be indispensable for protecting delicate human eyes and minds. Delicate in their grasp of actuality. Protected from the sun or the light of God only by several layers of ambiguity.

Knowledge pours down through a funnel, as it were. From pure light into artless nature; from nature into fine art; from pictures into the pictorial characters of language (phonetic words were pre-dated by hieroglyphs); and finally, it trickles through words down into symbolization at its most refined—numerals. Progressively, through each segment of the funnel's narrowing, down-to-earth

Mexico: Trip 3

reference is more universally rendered to humans. Even as their perspective on the original source of wholly meaningful Light gets more restricted.

Unchanging, above all these human filters of perception, abides the absolute mystery of light and the rest of nature, of existence. Why, rather than nothing, is there anything—such as light? Whether one identifies it as an alternating wave of magnetism and electricity or as God.

Whatever. In the funnel of knowledge, visual arts would amount to a higher-level depiction of light than language. Hence, the more literates and mathematicians who value either artworks or Earth's natural environment, the better—the more spiritual, perhaps. Though letters or numbers be more practical for ordinary human affairs than direct depictions of colored light.

Language can also mark the light, though, in its own way, through words like "illumination." Which refers to seeing the ultimate truth, waking up to see the Light. Language, to a degree, can also mediate the finite and the infinite. Without words attached, human concepts like God and the laws of science remain unconscious or forgettable to most. Words are active in human memory: they classify substance, set emotion in motion, and then help transmit both data and feeling to others.

Most thinking, all talking, and all writing are uses of language. The Light enters human consciousness somewhat demystified on words, powered by curiosity and, occasionally, aesthetic feeling. (As it does, more mysteriously, on visual art or through nature, powered by aesthetic feeling and, occasionally, curiosity.) Through the consumption or construction of language, light stimulates the desire to obtain enlightenment, would be another way of putting it.

Science sacrifices much language illumination to the precision of numerals. And that gets results. Heavy users of numbers—scientists, technicians, and businesspeople, underneath the funnel—toss out a combination of down-to-earth benefits and detriments. They yield artificial mutations, good or bad, but short on meaning either way. For a new technology, whether it makes living more pleasant and lengthy, or unbearable and short, will not illuminate life. And neither does scientific cosmology, so far.

Think by the numbers excessively, and one is apt to forget that God exists above one's funnel. Yet scientific theory and research may, nonetheless, be seen as a mode of theology. As a like effort to understand—and incidentally influence—the universe. That being principally attempted with mathematical symbols or geometric models substituting for words or pictures—and for rites, it has scientific method.

In the same way, less-theoretical pursuits that try highlighting the world's loveliness and wonder

Mexico: Trip 3

could be theistic, too. The arts could be seen as forms of worship, artists as God-inspired seers, and art-lovers as their congregations. Among whom many make offerings of money to their gods of light. Or they buy painted or sculpted household gods. Or they buy outdoor equipment and supplies for a wilderness pilgrimage through natural light. Or they buy all required tickets to approach famous tourist idols. By which they give to the Church of Art. But all day long, the Light, Itself, down hot rays, overspreads all creation for free. And some presume It is immanent, too.

Emphasizing light itself as an integral component of the godhead is a view poles apart from the medieval church conviction that appearances below are nothing more than indications of an ideal order somewhere else: heaven. A transcendent God being the only significant reality. But ask any pantheist, and he or she will tell you that the primary existence omnipresent on Earth, "nature," is unidentified deity. Further, that the entities on Earth that light illuminates, themselves, are all aspects of that deity—the real Thing.

Many ancient peoples, including the Egyptians, Persians, and Peruvians, went in for sun worship. In these primitive, more pragmatic religions, the sun mostly stood for fertility, though. Its magic made their crops thrive and thereby supported the continuance of their race. But a desert religion debuting now in Baja might come out different—playing up the fertile imaginations of artists and surfers more than farmers. A peninsula of sparkling grittiness piercing a deep of sparkling brine: the geographical finger of the Lord. A fitting scene for surfing or starting a sun cult.

Zeke wasn't a surfer, but he checked into a motel room in Todos Santos. Then, on his way back to it from the galleries, he tottered on the brink of an unfilled swimming pool, rather than a comber. Its lip ran along the patio before all first-floor room doors. Mind awash in obscurity, as usual, he lurched to a headlong halt close before wiping out in a bone-breaking belly flop into the deep end. As at gaping pitfalls along other pathways of that developing nation, there was no safety fencing. Two chained dogs bayed mournfully across the street.

Sierra de la Laguna Biosphere Preserve

The track into there began alongside a stream. But Zeke's two-quart canteen was almost full. Higher in the hills, the same meandering stream was crossed twice more, and then came a stagnant tributary. By then his canteen was about half empty, but that rivulet was rank. An iodine tablet could have made it potable, yet he felt disinclined to carry the weight of gunky water in his pack. After so many stream crossings, a good-enough one still ahead seemed probable.

Due to his goof in La Paz, his map showed the trail from maybe only a mile beyond the height of land above him. There it showed water, but not how close he was. Alas, before the last of about five shadeless, thirsty miles uphill, Zeke's canteen ran dry. Soon, he was undergoing heart palpitations while at rest—initial symptom of heat exhaustion. He choked down a salt tablet. **(26)**

Now came pangs of regret at passing up that last cruddy water. Which lumped together with fretting about whether he was on the correct trail and, if so, whether the water signified on his map flowed year-round. So that, to conserve strength and time, he hid his pack and quick-marched upward, his muscles fueled by fright. "*Water!*" What a relief to see liquid there! The fear of water deprivation is deep-rooted and almighty. **(27)**

Clear water cascading through a split-level meadow. Miniature brown frogs, slimy tadpoles, and water striders lived in it—sure signs of purity. A sandbar lay beneath, with flecks of mica glittering like gold. Orange dragonflies hovered. As Zeke drank about a pint and relaxed, his aesthetic sensibility switched on again. It only needed watering.

He camped. Next day there were two small beige hawks flying low above the waterless lakebed grassland. There were two foot-long lizards with green heads, yellow neck bands, gray-green tails, and yellow dots. There were two large bushes of pink blossoms. And downstream, at the grassland's end, there was one high waterfall into deep, rocky pools.

Going back to his tent, no longer thirsty but hungry for dinner, he began to conceive his environment as salad. Greenery from several ordinarily discrete zones all tossed together, way high in a bowl on an arid tabletop mountain. Overweight crotons had rolled downhill inward from its rim: boulders with yellowish-green-brown moss. You just add oil and vinegar. Dark through dawn, however, the contents of the bowl, including his sleeping bag, went into the refrigerator.

Which further brought to mind:

> The same as with tasting a meal, while taking in the scenery walking, a custom of perception may open up. Through pausing often to thoroughly sample the flavor of your present repast outspread, to let pure sensations warm your cold pot of past- or future-oriented daydreams.

Going down, at one trail turn, flourishing in temperate ocean breezes were: pines with mossy branches; varieties of tall live oaks, some with red leaves; big madrones; a few palms. Plus, there grew a prominent white-barked *palo blanco* letting on it was birch.

> Giving nature his mind muffled Zeke's compulsion to repetitiously run cliché reverie and old jokes to himself. A mental complaint that had plagued him off-and-mostly-on since childhood.

Farther was a chaparral belt with scattered Cape live oaks, manzanita, and piñon pines. Where the other day, pausing, exhausted, with sticky dry mouth, hearkening for water, Zeke was startled when a hummingbird dove at him or his red shirt. They were green, with dull-yellow masks. And the climate at that elevation was hummingbird heaven, judging by their abundance. But there were also impish ravens croaking, raucous jays, and little gray-olive birds wearing gaudy reddish-brown crests, like wigs. Two turkey buzzards circled him hopefully where he reclined, where the far-flung seashore's tan sandhills with white arroyos met his gaze.

Mexico: Trip 3

Downhill some more, the desert zone's ambition was to burgeon into tropical jungle. Organ-pipe cacti, some with white flowers open in morning, often grew up from the roots of trees; choking them like plump, multi-headed green snakes. Thornscrub, which razor-slashed flesh, was there, too; as were low, lichen-splotched, smooth, gray, *talisay* trees with dying orange leafage; and saplings hung with dense mats of sere, beige vines; and golf balls of gray epiphyte moss on branches; and bushes of daisy-style yellow flowers; and high, spindly bushes with split pods dangling like icicles; and yellow poppies with tiny red centers—bee bulls-eyes. All present and accounted for as a wild fig, with creepy roots, devoured boulders near the watercourse.

> On earth his eye was always selective. He couldn't focus on everything. Always there persisted a background of inattention within his field of vision. Yet, see enough somethings in this reality, and it's at least an approach to seeing everything.

In the air were black-and-orange tiger butterflies; black butterflies with pale-blue wing outlines; black bumblebees; wasps; small yellow butterfly swarms above the dust. And on the ground were black lizards, and brown-gray ones with steel-blue tails and long yellow pinstripes. There, on a lost-world upland, birds and lizards reigned—many models of economy-size dinosaur. A constant cooing of doves composed the background. While at dusk were seen two eagles with woodpecker-like streamlined crests. The type of raptor that appears on the Mexican flag with a snake in its beak. And with the red setting sun's light fading, a gray fox ran away.

Mexico: Trip 3

As who wouldn't be, Zeke was more than ready to slumber in his van. It was parked about ten miles from pavement, up a byway sandy enough to go one-on-one with any two-wheel drive. So he wasn't expecting company, but wouldn't you know it! Soon two SUV loads of adults and teenagers with quite a few children pulled in by a well-worn fire circle not far enough away. A boom box began broadcasting Mexican pop, so cheerfully singsong. 1-2-3, 1-2-3, accordion and guitar, second-rate mariachi. (Melodic ballads from Broadway musicals and even vocal jazz were heard in some Mexican beaneries. Rock seldom, beyond the Beatles and moldy '50s tunes.)

After a lengthy spell of drunken ruckus, the music broke off, bottles smashed into the underbrush, and they were off for the highway, passing many sun-faded "No Tire Basura" signs. But their campfire was left to go out on its own. It was burning low, even at get-up time, when Zeke got wind of it. The heat was on for the tinder-dry World Biosphere. He'd witnessed those yokels' regular Sunday evening routine, like as not. Within Mexico's pop culture, vanilla rock and staying home to watch television might represent progress. Fortunate for Zeke, it was, that he didn't get toasted like a hard taco shell in his sleep.

He was too drained when he first came down from the biosphere to think back on his brush with dehydration the previous day; or the sweaty climb that brought it on. Only driving out did he fully appreciate that it was a missing topographic map that gave rise to his inept hiking plan. With more idea of the trail's length, rather than tote his entire backpack up, he could have cached it near the last pure curve of the watercourse, seen the topside in good time with only a day pack, and then come down to camp same-place below, missing out on the Sunday wilderness schmaltz fest, too. **(28)**

Todos Santos

He checked into a different motel for a shower. Soon thereafter, a red rash erupted on his crotch. Why? From having worn a swimsuit, then put it out to dry off without rinsing. Then, in about a week, wearing it again. So much for his assumption that fungus finds no foothold on the airy, nylon-mesh lining of a swimsuit. **(29)**

Slipping into filthy habits is convenient while living out of a suitcase or pack. Anyhow, slipping out of passably clean ones is. Cleanliness is simplified by familiar circumstances or, sometimes, by home paraphernalia too bulky to pack. Therefore, needed habits to secure freedom from impurities should be scrupulously acquired while living at one address awhile. Since merely bringing to mind brushing your teeth gets to be more demanding while on the move.

Keeping to the ordinary run of things at home, nevertheless, can straitjacket resourcefulness through its sameness. While abroad, your habits must be more flexible. Being caught up in many untried twists and turns, as they are. Indeed, it was dealing with this baffling array of new problems that set Zeke to writing his imperatives on underwear control, and so forth.

Some troubles defy all adjustment, howsoever, besides escape. Promptly next morning, the management began serving decibels for breakfast in bed. Zeke hopped out and opened the curtain to behold a steamroller smoothing new paving in the auto court. It went "ARRRRRRR...!" for as long as he had to stand it, like a wearing habit.

Puerto Algodones (!!!)

Aquamarine sea trimmed with white splashing against the gray-black cove. Coming down from the barren ridge behind, he had the idea at first: "swimmers' heads." Closer, they changed into birds. A drift of some twenty-five brown-backed, white-bellied pelicans, gliding and diving near the briny pond's edge. And rising offshore was their nesting rock, streaked with white.

A wave-worn stone dock was his front row amphitheater seat for pelican ballet—a real performance. Bird watching beyond name-dropping can be the unobstructed spectacle of graceful fowl with top billing in coordinated motion, throughout a sunny, calm sea cove. Whether sitting tall on shore or coasting above the billows, their enactment had an ageless feel. Pterodactyls! Swooping down even now, gliding before a backdrop of black and shaded lava, hedgehopping or diving, mostly in unison, out over their liquid stage. And when a white-headed juvenile pelican caught and gulped a fish, its bill pouch gleamed bright pink.

There were a few grebes in the water, too. Black snakes on end with pointed noses, they resembled. Then, at noon, a half-dozen buzzards came soaring high, crosswise over the cove's sky. White feathers posterial upon their wings, black and white underneath, with fleshy red heads. **(30)**

A school of silvery 2-ft. fish were barely perceptible beneath the foam. On the rock skittered a black crab, which is to say, a jumbo stalk-eyed sea spider. It hid in the shadow of Zeke's day pack and then jumped out to scare him when he reached for it, the little devil. Dead ones, turned ceramic orange with white dots, had eyes like burnt-out car headlights. Live, wet, and close, they had pretty black dots on their blue-gray carapaces, with orange along their forefronts and where their legs joined. More skittish than lizards, and every bit as watchful. Departing, he heard a seal barking, presumably, from out in a sub-cove 'round a rocky corner from his crumbling dock.

Punta San Pedro [Playa San Pedrito]

Here, there were three pronounced facets: the full-grown coconut grove behind; the brackish lagoon walled off by dunes, with green plants and birds; the beach bounded by sharp, gray, volcanic spines on both sides. The dissimilarity of its natural features held more eye interest than most seashore.

The beach: tan marbled with black sand stripes and splotches, like a pale tie-dyed pattern on cloth. The aquamarine bay: a dirty tan in broad expanses behind white breakers from sediment churned up offshore, with an unceasing muffled roar, and cliffs hacked from the volcanic rocks at their base by constant wave action.

The lagoon: metallic blue, with brown shallows; green reeds with brown tufts; higher cane thickets; orange dragonflies and bitty blue-gray ones; pint-size hawks, beige with black markings; two white egrets; sandpipers, tan with white bellies, flowing on short legs along the deep sea's fringes; a healthy flock of lustrous, chocolate-brown ducks, with their

Mexico: Trip 3

tan mates; a few coots; a pelican. A blue heron flapped up upon a tall cactus for safety. After a moment, it lifted itself off into the air with a single silent stroke of its great wings. A pelican skeleton lay on the bank.

There were columns of cacti separating off the lagoon and beach. Also, a patch of spiraling, long, gray cactus, making a 5-ft. hedge of prickly balloon critters. Gangling yellow daisies. A devil's claw caught Zeke's boot—a rude spring trap, with four curving, sharp, flexible prongs; large burrs gone high-tech.

The palm grove: many mature ones, about three stories high; doves little bigger than sparrows; black butterflies; a succulent with high stocks of yellow flowers.

Behind the palm grove lay a fine ruin: a sugarcane *rancho* with whitewashed, plastered lower story, scaling to brown, with a red brick upper story. Inside were log ceiling beams, a tile floor, a chapel under the stairs with bare altar and icon niche. Its collapsing flat roof was braced with two thick palm trunks. A second-floor wooden footbridge led to a smaller brick building behind. A corner of timeworn high brick wall, yet upright in the yard, was matted with magenta bougainvillea.

Next morningtide buzzards huddled on the beach. A pelican had a short length of fishing line taut through its lower bill, its other end tied to a hook in its chest. Zeke approached it with pliers and scissors, but it would flap away. Starving was in the cards, and then the buzzards would get it. On the lagoon were two long-legged waterfowl—white, black, and tan. What were they? One trailed a long cord looped above a splay-foot as it flew off. Some fishermen along that coast, between fish, amuse themselves with the birds. Explain why, in the last analysis, cruelty to birds feels worse than cruelty to fish.

According to a tourist agency brochure, this beach would soon be developed as a piece of a 1,100-acre "mega-resort" that would "change the area." Zeke could just see it. Bursting upon the view like "The Corridor" resorts near Cabo San Lucas. Trimmed, spongy green lawns and low bougainvillea with neat flowering shrubs enclosing smallish, blue cement swimming pools and cement walkways. A few palms surviving near glassy, nondescript, six-story hotel buildings. The *rancho* demolished. Or wait—instead, pile all that flat high-rise out near the highway, not along the beach. There, close behind a strip mall, to catch the swish and growl of traffic—music to merchants' ears, rousing background rumble for the guests. Then, pave the track all the way to the beachfront, and fill in the lagoon for a parking lot.

Cabo San Lucas

In Cabo, booksellers and tourist information staff were stumped by Zeke's descriptions of a tide table. Nevertheless, as knowing the tides is of importance for skin diving and other ocean sports, he persisted asking around. Eventually, the American expatriate manager of an RV park, an air pilot taking early retirement, knew about when the next low tide would come. Zeke supposed that was the best he'd get there. Even though Cabo San Lucas is one of Mexico's major beach and fishing resorts. **(31)**

Mexico: Trip 3

Bahia Santa Marta [Bahia Chileno]

Down the coast, Santa Marta was a formerly atmospheric cove, with fancy houses now built amazingly close to the tidewater. Still and all, it had an okay little beach from which to snorkel in good time, before sunbathers descended. Or so it seemed that fateful morning, as submarine Zeke, his periscope deployed, navigated one perimeter of the inlet.

His sonar ears glided under the chilly ocean blue, no longer irritated by the barking guard dog ashore; cruising above narrow flows of solidified lava divided by sunken troughs of sand. Muscling his swim strokes and kicks, he was, over strange crystalline flakes of color on the seabed, like yellow-to-orange stained glass in shards. What was farther out—a drowned church? A bloated brown puffer warned him away, and then another, blue with white dots.

After the third old lava flow, something was wrong. Zeke noticed the tide was dragging him out to sea more rapidly than he recovered by swimming with incoming swells. It stressed him. Making an all-out effort against it, he swallowed water. Which then made him distinctly afraid. Taken by surprise by the ocean!

Just then, his sub commander came over the intercom with calm seriousness: "Surface! Don't panic. Look around you." Zeke swept his eyes over the water; saw a black thing to his left. New orders: "Roll on your back and float with the out-tide. Swim for that rock in synch with incoming waves. Don't sink." The commander liked puns!

After what felt a long stretch, he grabbed onto a low crag of reef over which breakers were breaking. It lay about ten yards off the outer cove's sheer rock face. The next breaker nearly tore him off. His legs came loose. At which, sprawling over the sharp-edged lava, he tightened his grip with fingers, knees, and toes. Clinging like a starfish; imagining a starfish, underneath the crash and suck of whitecaps.

Fear, but no pain. Three or four more surges broke while he gulped air and looked to shore between them. His strength was ebbing faster than the tide. So right after the next one, he up and leapt at the lava wall, swam briefly, then, nimble-footed as a crab, scrambled rock to upgrade his position.

Touch and go, touch and go, climbing and boulder-hopping in time with swells to the beach. Where at last he stood trembling, and not only from the cold sea but also from residual adrenalin. He assessed his damage: a sprained thumb with purple nail; an aching elbow; minor lacerations on arms, legs, torso, and one finger; holes in his skin diving gloves and water shoes.

Sunbathers began coming to rest on the smallish beach in force about ten, but Zeke didn't care. Reclined against a boulder, enjoying the unitive pleasures of his body and mind, both releasing tension. Feeling way down how lucky it is to be alive. Still living! There's nothing like it—accept no substitute. (32)(33)

San Jose del Cabo

More sense of place held out than in Baja's other cities, but the fiesta honoring the town's patron saint had gone twenty-first-century. The main plaza's PA system blared so strong that Zeke's park bench shook. Oppressive, modulating, male

Mexico: Trip 3

announcer's vivacious tones penetrated everywhere downtown, like a nonstop commercial for cheerfulness. Mostly it traded volume for any sincere gaiety. None were buying it.

The girl dancers on stage wore national dress. The boys, barely childish enough to come on as more cute than ridiculous, wore authentic high-heeled boots, shorts, and T-shirts with garish California-style lettering and logos. One titillating dance featured the boys crouching low to the stage and looking up their partners' dresses as they twirled. So that an uncultured spectator might suspect this folksy folly was picked with an eye to luring boys to dance class. At wearing sissy old Spanish clothes, nonetheless, they balked—except the boots. And, upon closer inspection, the bandana-waving girls had on jeans or shorts under their lax skirts.

At the hotel desk, Zeke graciously yielded his turn on the phone to an overwrought American anxious to call the airport about missing tickets. Their baggage had been stolen from their car, he explained. Their tickets were in it. Meantime, his wife chattered nervously on and on without pause, to the lady receptionist, pointedly ignoring her spouse. Her focus of attention implying that she felt he was to blame but wouldn't say so, leastways not in the lobby. Perhaps they were on their honeymoon.

According to the clerk, when at last she spoke, crime was exploding in Mexico. Which might account for the country estates along the coast fortified with high chainlink fences overtopped with barbed wire—two complete rings of fence enclosing some. And it may have accounted for the many barking upscale yard dogs, too. Fear or mistrust were becoming prominent and noisy around both rural and suburban dwellings in Baja.

Zeke was only pinched by dishonesty of any kind in San Jose, at a Cooks' traveler's check exchange booth. Where, soon before closing one day, because they hadn't posted one, he asked and was quoted their rate. Next day, though, when he forgot to ask again till after the moneychanger scrawled on his check, the exchange rate had apparently slipped. Though the closed bank next door had kept *its* posted rate unchanged. In place of an explanation, Zeke got a speedy mark-cooling recitation about the rate of pesos for dollars as opposed to its reverse. Totally beside the point and with overdone garbling, but as the difference was under two dollars, Zeke let it go.

On previous Mexican shopping adventures, though, he was often perturbed by the readiness of rats in trade to overcharge less-assertive consumers—among them, foreign mice. Then he more or less got used to it and countered by picking stores with price tags on everything. Does gypping mice out of small sums qualify as a sneakier sort of machismo? **(34)(35)**

Bahia Pulmo National Marine Park

At Playa La Serinita, a shallow sandy cove, were pale sea-sculpted rocks going out into the tide like a string of low horns, goring the blue. Also an elongated mound of big oval rocks, dappled black, like monster waterfowl eggs. Otherwise

Mexico: Trip 3

the strand was more like a boneyard than a rookery: white coral skeletons, animal bones, pelican bones, orange crab shells, sun-bleached scraps of seashell (clam bone).

Cold water. The coral was less colorful than in warmer seawater—mossy olive or gray mostly. Or was it so from pollution? A multicolor world of fish swam, anyhow: poky starfish overloaded with stubby arms; thin, nearly transparent pipefish; roly-poly porcupine puffers. With white dots on brown, black, or blue, those same seductive Santa Marta sirens. These plus all the usual suspects: parrot fish, butterfly fish, clown fish, etc. etc. fish.

Swimming the rock-studded shoreline en route to a far-off parking beach, Zeke confronted two moray eels in separate locations. Both were whipping along above the seabed rather than lying undercover as might be expected. One turned on him and menaced with wide open jaws, but only that. Not all fierce fish boldly attack on sight, like hungry sharks. Even some sharks are nicer than others! A pretty nurse shark lay partially under cover of white chipped-coral particles, much like a flounder; pale-yellow skin with black polka dots, head broad and rather cone-shaped. Lying in a gap among strips of coral, it was surely too tranquil to bite without provocation. (Only 2 or 3 ft. long.)

Zeke got out at Playa Traffic Noise. Many natives going fishing went in for maneuvering their vehicles onto the beach, though there was a dirt parking lot of sorts. It set Zeke to theorizing why. Perhaps to avoid theft. Wait—to prove their macho skill at driving on uncertain sand! Dah . . . how about prestige? Or to imitate TV commercials with the all-new

1982 Toyota dislocating a natural scene. Then it came to him. How hot lethargy combines with safeguarding against the dangers of nature in the raw. Hulking protective machines an easy walk or sprint from their *palpa* mini-castles were just how average desert-dwellers liked engaging with a thorny, thirsty environment.

Mexico is mostly desert. In such a milieu, autos are a godsend. Hence, car idolatry possibly surpasses even that met with in the land of their origin. Which is why there were black T-shirts in La Paz store windows printed with portrayals of Jesus wearing a bleeding crown of thorns, hovering above a customized pickup truck. (Signifying the unconscionable expense of extra chrome?) Other T-shirts had the Madonna above a motto supplicating her protection from traffic accidents.

Roman Catholicism came from Spain. Have Mexicans more lately imported a new creed from North America: Orthodox Automobilism? Is Detroit replacing Jerusalem in their hearts? Just as some elements of older pagan creeds, and original contributions, were grafted by the Tarahumara and others onto Christianity as it spread, now may emerge newer grafts as it retrogresses—a familiar historical process in reverse gear. A new version of faith, fabricated in a new desert, as old-model Christianity backs up and gets stuck in sinking sand.

A notice in the parking lot prohibited beach parking. "These scofflaws must stand condemned by society!" Zeke fantasized thundering at the top of his lungs, before remembering himself. "Right! And a law against fishing would also be nice" was his second reaction. There were fishermen galore on the shore, but few fish in the reef compared to the less-accessible cove where

Mexico: Trip 3

he launched forth. "A natural ecosystem despoiled! Our planet plundered!" (Not to mention the detriment to skin diving.) It tickled Zeke's sense of righteousness or political propriety, led his associations, to bestow critical thought upon ecological issues at every provocation. (Anyway, someone had to, for the good of humanity. Global warming having graduated from hypothesis to scientific principle in the past decade.)

But come to think of it, truth be known, sea creatures of these waters had worse problems than shore fishing. The narrow sliver of protected seashore along its access road was undergoing a construction boom. Now sewage from homes and resorts, just across the way from parkland, was swiftly polluting into oblivion that which drew the less asphalt- or fish-hungry there. In their homey or touristy ways, they were endangering the biosphere, at the one and only coral reef in the Sea of Cortez.

Zeke saw a pattern:

> The human species increases, causing reef fish, coral, and beaches devoid of parked cars to decrease. Therefore, "No parking" notices are put up. Now extrapolate this observation from beaches to all other resources of the global ecosystem. To protect resources and wealth, more population requires more regulation. A state of affairs that sheds light on the shocking proliferation of public rules, from codes of conduct down to hardcore laws that dictate stern punishments. A population explosion sets off a collateral boom in social control. It beefs up the multiplicity and consequence of lawyers, bureaucrats,

law enforcement, and other sticklers for the norm. It adds up to The Age of Prisons (along with famine, war, pestilence, and so forth).

"A good traveler is one who does not know where he is going to, and a perfect traveler does not know where he came from. He does not even know his own name." —Lin Yutang

(Zen or Alzheimer's?)

Laws or commands mean taking orders—being told what to do or not, and when to do it or not. Then, qualms about domination make rules of behavior and agendas unpopular. They being associated with parental discipline, school, job, or police—with bending minds into conformity, with bossing. Zeke, since before his teens, was overmuch prickly about complying with minor regulations, having noted by then that he was too much of a born follower already to suit his aspirations.

That was why Zeke's adult practice got to be making up standard operating procedures and agendas for himself that, if obeyed, could reduce his exposure to both ruling institutions and imperfect, conventional wisdom. Directions for getting away, mostly they were—for spending more quality time with Mother Nature. By way of improving his efficiency at doing typical disagreeable tasks connected with penetrating and subsisting with her, along with instructions for improving physical security or comfort. Paradoxical, it was. A special-case dislike for others' guidelines led him to write a body of new ones on his own.

Those who might consider Zeke a daring outlaw, anarchist, nut—they exaggerate some. A dedicated traveler who

Mexico: Trip 3

out-of-the-way went on shortcuts and mapped them, yes. For the more a mouse can save time, money, and suffering, he realized, the farther that mouse will go. And the longer s/he will walk in beauty. While as a bonus, the austerity involved in complying with instructions based ultimately upon their prior deviations and stupidities should keep them humble.

His belief:

> Independent travel is more roundabout than doing an everyday job, loaded with instabilities and problems hard to deal with. So cues on adapting to it yet allow substantial room for offhand response. As with artists, who save and concentrate creative energy through routinizing as much of their daily preparation and execution as possible, so travelers may also benefit from ripening their technique.
>
> Travel technique produces no automatism. Forgetfulness and pitfall variations see to that. And whenever a travel pointer seems too narrow for circumstances, what fun to off-and-on misbehave and see what happens! (After which, revision of a standing rule is more often productive than scrapping it entirely.)
>
> God and other authorities have contrived a world so labyrinthine as to admit almost unlimited opportunity for fresh, unpredictable error and misfortune. Yet they also allow their opposite: improbable successes and strokes of luck. Only to make the delusion of free will more persuasive, suspicious losers may brood . . .

Mexico: Trip 3

In any event, carefree goers who completely let themselves go, relaxing all self-control, relying upon their impulses, flying by the seat of their pants—they generally wind up going in circles, seeing the same shops or bars over and over. For it is forethought overruling impulse that separates humans from animals, and travelers from compulsive shoppers or drunkards. Selection favors creatures who plan how and where to proceed. Long trips outside your head make instructions indispensable for going places—as much as they are for conservation, cooking, or staging a drama. Instructions on how best to proceed.

Even such painfully acquired wisdom as not exposing fair skin for too long to a tropical sun was forethought over and above for dopey Zeke that day at Bahia Pulmo. He lay face down on the salty ocean's surface longer than his lotion lay on his back. Afterwards, to keep his skin from itching, he finessed a gratis outdoor shower from a handy dive shop. During which, a swimsuited gentleman lugging scuba gear, who still managed to look like a doctor, and spoke with a German accent to heighten the effect, asked about the scrapes on Zeke's side left over from the Santa Marta mishap. "Kissed by the reef," was his parting comment. Although facing Zeke, as he was, made him unable to examine Lobsterman's cooked dorsal region. "Blushing at the sun goddess's caress," or even "Groped by the sun." So a pro snorkeler might have diagnosed his condition there. (36)(37)(38)(39)

Mexico: Trip 3

Los Barriles—La Paz

Next morning, about a third of the way on the roads north to La Paz, Zeke spied breakfast in a California-cloned strip mall. Baja got so massive a migration of both North Americans and Europeans in winter that orderly, clean, uninspiring rows of consistent architecture sprang up along the highways of beach towns and cities like weeds. Or cottonwoods?

Formerly, cottonwood tufts drifted down from the fertile U.S. mercantile woodlands to the north, and into some Mexican trading posts. By this twenty-first century visit of Zeke's, though, strip malls wholly intact were gravitating out of Gringoland—uprooted saplings, thumping down and taking root in Mexican soil. Moreover, if knock-offs of entire North American retail buildings with their contents could proliferate in Baja, they might hit soil conditions as propitious in other sunny southern realms farther afield. Given help by expats and tourists from the north, who go anywhere sunny to perform their role as cultivators or manure-spreaders.

So the United States, with all its busy bee migrant population for hybrid pollination, serves as an experimental merchandising arboretum. In various ethnic soils testing to find what hybrid saplings are most suitable for cultural cultivation in new lands. No more slash-and-burn colonialism: matured transplants imported from a relatively multicultural plantation, and with tourists coming much more often than permanent colonists.

Playa Balandra

A long inlet, shallow enough as the tide went out for sandbars to show in the middle. Tide flow imprinted with a crisscross design. The rising sea was emerald green. Zeke waded over the curious, ridged-sand bottom in chest-high water, feeling its texture under his toes.

Enclosing the inlet sat low dunes below arid hills sprouting a few cacti. Seclusion there was on the far shore, hemmed in landward by sweet-smelling mangrove thickets. Neither Mexican teenagers nor adults would often set foot in the sea. There nor elsewhere. A taboo kept alive by hazardous currents on some beaches, such as Santa Marta.

Violet, rust, green, and red coral covered sizable rocks off the farther shore. Most of the smaller fish from Bahia Pulmo made the scene. There were many starfish and brilliant crabs. On a rock pile in the cove's narrow mouth, some of the birds seen at Punta San Pedro were also there: a great blue heron flew away, a frigate bird with long drooping tail perched.

La Paz—Juncalito— Loreto—San Javier

While driving south a few weeks previous, Zeke had intended to see San Javier mission, up a twenty-two mile unpaved side road from the coastal highway. But the night before came a dream. After rousing, he could only bring back its last fragment. A red item or light, perhaps on his dashboard, was shining as his van backed up. That was it. But of more concern than its content was an emotional coloring of dread that accompanied it into his awakening mind.

Subconsciously, the image yet resonated close to recollection as he lay in the sack. An interpretation came on. The dashboard light might signify that making the run to San Javier would cause such a breakdown as to prevent him making it to

Mexico: Trip 3

the cape. That did it. He invoked a long-standing ominous-dream rule of his and made up his mind, there and then, to skip the detour. He'd do it maybe on the way back. **(40)**

Now camping at Juncalito again, on his way north, Zeke awoke with no memory trace of any unusual dream. So he had a mind to try the mission's road this time by. Had the image that stopped him before alluded to his carburetor trouble approaching La Paz? A severe loss of power that made getting over the final hills before town poky and uncertain? But he couldn't remember a red light shining then, or going in reverse, either. Never mind—now his heap was set to rights and running fine.

The dirt road went sharply downhill in some sections and there was a wide stream to ford, but overall it held less risk of sticking in grit than, for instance, the one to Sierra de la Laguna. He reached San Javier mission without incident.

It sat in a high bowl of desert mountain ridges. Which made it seem smaller than it was. A late-medieval, domed, semi-gothic church, with fading whitewash; its inner air was chill and laden with the flat scent of stale, sweet incense. Behind it was one gnarly olive tree, old as the church, and a small assortment of fruit trees. All over the oasis vale were irrigated vegetable gardens, but the presence of barbed wire and barking dogs prevailed.

In the foreground, it looked as if some set designer on a tight budget had once tried to revive the exteriors on part of its village. Presumably, before or after the shooting of *The Magnificent Seven* with Yul Brenner. In preparation for the scene during which he and six other reformed rats shot a host of Mexican bandits. (After having first taken the diplomatic precaution of locally enlisting a few of their humble peasant victims on the side of the good guys.)

By the street to the church façade were a block of whitewashed huts with thatched roofs, but the street itself was filled with a raised strip of cement, embedded with wide-set token cobblestones. With barren cement planters along its verges and rows of streetlamps it was meant to appear old-fashioned, but in fact looked new and out-of-place—the afterthought of some uninspired bureaucrat?

At the far end of the funny restoration, the cement up and quit, just like that. Below the resulting step, more than a foot high, the original street then resumed, wending its way by a trash dump on the bank of a polluted stream. It all came down to slipshod restoration and population pressure blighting a once-beautiful site. Fortunately, there had been another green canyon valley halfway back, and to that Zeke hastened.

Las Parras Oasis/Loreto Bay Marine Park

This canyon oasis was much more elongated than the one by San Juan de Magdalena road, also deeper. A relic stretch of an outworn dirt and cobble carriageway to the mission led into it.

Fig saplings grew from crevices in the reddish-brown canyon side. Fan palms below twinkled in the sun. A few date palms. Paloverde. Mesquite. Agave. Organ pipe cactus. Prickly pear. A weird cholla-like cactus with zigzag branches, like thick woven ropes. Sweet-smelling thorny brushwood in bloom with greenish-yellow catkins, luring black bees. At the

Mexico: Trip 3

upper end, an orchard: orange trees, olive trees, grape vines. Tall white poppies with yellow centers.

Quiet: only a trickling spring and doves cooing; a few croaking frogs; a few long brown lizards stirring; small orange-black butterflies, some with white dots along their wing fringes; and small yellow butterflies. Plus, sure as fate, Baja buzzards sweeping overhead.

The seashore where he slept the night before, south of the canyon mouth, had had a grove of lofty palms backed by pinnacles. From a nearby overlook, Loreto Bay Marine Park had outspread its rocky spines, rising near and far, out to the horizon, poking through a magic sea mirror of water-blink light. From Las Parras out through Loreto Bay and up the coast to Punta Candeleros would make a marvelous park. At what other locality in the natural world may be seen together oases, sheer ravine, palm beach, and drowned coast with rows of stark rocks offshore interspersed with uninhabited keys?

On the way out, Zeke came to the steep hill that had given him grief coming in. Near its middle, a big, flat rock jutted out at too acute an angle for even a high-clearance vehicle. Tricky to get by. It took braking lightly on unstable gravel and rock downhill, left tires running near the edge of a 200-ft. precipice. There was not enough room on the other side, short of a ditch below boulders, to get over much.

Now, the up climb was even trickier, without taking it so rashly as to risk lurching off loose stones over the brink. On his uphill run, fighting gravity, his front wheels bounced off rocks until, slowed, his rear ones began digging into sandy gravel. On too narrow a lane for safe turning around. Then, while benefiting from the slope to free his wheels and back down, braking in reverse, there came a new threat. Once he braked, and the van slid sideways over a foot toward the brink, ceasing just in time.

Zeke parked below the hill. He began pacing upward on the washed-out road, surveying it. "Not a chance." Before getting far, however, there unexpectedly bobbed over the crest and came downhill a husky, suntanned man wearing shorts, a blue shirt, and wraparound shades. He asked whether Zeke spoke Spanish or Italian. "No." Then, in barely intelligible English and sign language, interspersed with Italian, the newcomer asked if Zeke had seen his companions, in a jeep. "No." But in a sudden fit of extroversion, Zeke then tried to convey having seen scarcely anyone all day on that road, but that lately he'd been hiking off it. (A fellow outdoorsman.) And what's more, that now he couldn't manage this hill in his van down there. (Implying, "Help!")

Graciously, the Italian proposed that he guide him up by waving. That got him no higher than before. Once more his tires caught in deep gravel near the cliff edge, a couple yards below the obstacle. Then, at the hill's base again, a red jeep drove by. It came to a stop above the stumbling block on a flatter grade. (4-wheel drive.) The Italian trotted up to it and then signaled for Zeke. In answer to whether he had a tow rope, Zeke went and got his nylon hiking cord, but it wouldn't do. A yellow jeep arrived.

Next, his Italian friend suggested undertaking the hill in Zeke's van himself. "*Sí*." He took it way back to the stream ford for more of a start. From which he was able to build up more speed than Zeke had. So, with that and more nerve, his outer wheels close to perdition at the crucial spot, he made it.

While trudging up again, with a very sincere *"Gracias!"* ready, a guy beside the yellow jeep gave Zeke a glare of scorn. Credibly, for taking advantage of his friend's or employee's nobility. But giving a brave man opportunity to demonstrate his virtue and driving skill might also be seen as a generous act, Zeke felt.

On the way out to pavement, Zeke reflected upon recent events. What were the odds that a plucky, benevolent pro racecar driver (or at any rate, experienced jeep driver) would come marching down this obscure, wild byway at precisely the moment when he needed him most? Exactly the man to keep from either being stranded there a long while or, about as likely, in crazed frustration taking on the killer hill flat-out, beyond his driving expertise, and after only a brief flight, crashing to his death. Was his guardian angel Italian, then, the same as most of the popes? And was the whole thing but one more example of God's special providence for fools?

Then there came to mind the dream fragment that he had a notion was a premonition a few weeks ago, which had him diverging from his itinerary then as per rule. Well, this afternoon's bad road had his car steering for deep trouble in reverse, and a ruby-red jeep, like a warning light! That dream *did* fill the bill back then as a garbled, composite vision of his startling skid while backing down Camino El Rocko earlier.

Mexico: Trip 3

The red jeep: like for "Danger!" or "Stop!" Zeke felt that his accustomed rational resistance to the idea of divine intervention, always weak, then and there, on that holy dirt road, had slipped a notch.

He felt protected—that was it. Divine order reigned! The Good Driver upstairs had cause to keep him alive until he had accomplished his mission here below. (Whatever that might turn out to have been when he reported back). His soul was now, and permanently had been, immortal. Receiving forewarnings up from their unconscious was special equipage for mortals whose brains, due to idiosyncratic-wiring irregularities, might not otherwise succeed in keeping them alive long enough to achieve their objectives on Earth.

The Italian jeeper and his pals would not have been there at the crucial juncture to save him had he gone out on the day of his forewarning! The holy computer upstairs in charge of scheduling made his oblivious mind switch from stop to go after precisely the correct nighttime. Zeke felt joy—a profound sense of power. Not so much from his escape, but rather out of new hope that he could now foretell his trajectory well enough to avoid all personal catastrophes that might lie in wait. (Drowning aside?)

It was more than 40 years into his introspection before Zeke became aware of his precognition. Did it grow more pronounced with age, or was he too credulously orthodox or unread when younger to admit premonitions? They first came to his attention as vivid, disturbing remnants of nightmares. And this remained for him their most recognizable form.

Subsequently, he also began taking an interest in distinctive kinds of daydream, too. Those that oddly preceded misadventures. Gentle hints that arose out of context with a thought in progress. Out of the blue, fleeting visual reruns of former hazards surmounted, but of the same sort as one then approaching, he would afterwards recognize. Or sometimes the hints were in scraps of songs or films that popped up. Low-key waking intuitions of trouble just ahead.

Day or night, though, his glimpses out of the present alluded only to imminent threat—never to desirable stuff coming his way. And not before all mishaps did they occur—only for some. (Were they often overlooked and forgotten?) Typically, he didn't heed them when they came on, grasping their significance only in retrospect. In fact, camped on that beach before trying the San Javier route was but the third time in memory that he prudently acted upon recognizable second sight to evade an unseen danger.

Zeke's mode of ESP, from out of the farther reaches of fear, argued a determined world, in which one's future circumstances already exist somewhere forward in time. Likewise, a world that somehow gave the go-ahead for a mind at times to see concealed perils in its near future and then dodge them. Furthermore, the incident on San Javier road also implied that, by heeding such intuitions only to the extent of delay, an agency able to give an assist in overriding the peril may come into play. That which went beyond good timing. But fitting it all into a decent system of metaphysics without hiding the loose ends behind personal destiny, theology, angels, and so on—that was beyond Zeke's reasoning.

Mulege

From the coast south of town, Zeke drove in for breakfast. The parking spaces near the plaza were all taken, but a few blocks farther along was one with almost enough room for two cars. So, to parallel park, he pulled in frontward rather than backing as usual. But then, as his front wheels neared the curb, there came the ugly metallic rasp and clank of tearing metal.

When Zeke got out to investigate, a liberated woman in a doorway across the street let off an hysterical shriek of laughter. For his rear bumper had hooked the tip of a VW Rabbit's bumper parked behind—wrenched it right off. A mass of headlight wiring dangled to the street like spilled intestines. While one end of the chrome bumper was still held up by his. *What have you done?* galloped into his mind, riding upon a remorse. *There* was one he didn't see coming.

The gap betwixt the curving end of a Dodge van bumper and its fender is little more than one inch. The VW's bumper was even tighter. And yet there was no scrape mark on the VW's finish. A persevering demolition-derby driver might have tried hours and scraped many fenders without matching Zeke's feat. A truly miraculous fender-bender, it was.

The Rabbit owner's brother or friend rushed out of a nearby establishment, squawking in Spanish. "You moron! What have you done to our car?" or suchlike. Then came the irate but more self-controlled owner, who mentioned the police. So Zeke made a sorrowful long sit on the curb. The police came. One officer rode with Zeke in his van to their office. From whence he was driven to a clinic and assigned some toe-to-heel toddling. By an English-speaking doctor

Mexico: Trip 3

when he finally got back from lunch, after another protracted delay. And Zeke was then asked about alcohol consumption.

He'd been cold sober through all of it—no excuse. (Other than not having had his morning coffee.) Cold sober! By then, without booze to ease his extra-snug frontal cortex, another mouse in his position might have been affected by nagging remorse, or leastways embarrassment. But Zeke was too scared of jail just then to feel much in the way of either for long. Also, he was hungry.

At their station again, the cops booked him and kept his car key. Zeke, however, was not locked up. So his anxiety subsided some. Only they warned him not to leave town before the nearest insurance-claims adjuster made his damage estimate. Señor claims adjuster lived in La Paz. So that gave Zeke sack time in his seized property over in the police parking lot. Which he soon used, exhausted after a long day of mental strain and sitting tight.

At dawn, when he awoke, a new anxiety struck. When was the expiration date on his Mexican auto-insurance policy? He took a peek. Over a week ago!

At the bank, when it opened, he went and cashed his last $350 in traveler's checks. His ATM account was already empty. The rest of the day, mostly whiling away time near the *playa*, the old Kingston Trio refrain from "Tijuana Jail" ran through his brain cells continually. "Just $500, and they'll set me free. I couldn't raise a penny, if you threatened me . . ." and so forth. His own financial plight and legal problem were similar, Zeke felt. Although he was much farther into Mexico than Tijuana.

Mexico: Trip 3

In late afternoon a hangdog Zeke slunk into the police station to inquire about any new developments in his case. ("Hang down your head, Tom Dooley!") There, a cop grabbed his arm tight to escort him into the chief's office, for the damage estimate had come. An unbelievably even $1,000 to reattach a dislocated but otherwise undamaged bumper and headlights. Plus, there was the $200 traffic fine for wrecking on a public thoroughfare or whatnot.

Zeke assured them that he would contact his auto-insurance firm during their open hours next day and then get back to them. The duty sergeant let go his arm. But, on second thought, back in his van, as gloom descended, Zeke hit upon an informal barter deal to settle his debt. Simple: they could keep his van. ($1,200, by chance, being almost the exact amount paid for it a few years previous. And its four nearly new, wide-track radial tires along with the new fuel pump covered depreciation, he felt. Yeah, that sounded about right.)

At first, there had been a Plan A: Use his duplicate car key to make a 615-mile dash for the line up Baja's only arterial road. Then go through immigration in his downwardly mobile automobile. But it didn't sound like safe driving. On to Plan B: There was a bus station only a couple blocks from his parking lot. There was one and only one going north that evening, within an hour. There was no time to reconsider, barely enough to pack.

Once at the station, an edgy ten-minute delay ensued. Running a bit late it was, that day. Anyway, good thing it hadn't started a bit too soon, as Mexican buses occasionally did. Zeke checked three bags but then didn't stick around to see them loaded, as was his established way. Only from down the street a piece did he keep the bus in sight. There being other things on his tense mind than baggage thieves: the forces of law and order.

But at least he was not guilt-ridden: the bus was. Guilty as a funky overdue bus can be, as it got underway with Zeke slouched on-board—guilty of aiding a fugitive. The same as his faulty, criminally negligent van in custody had been guilty the other day. How could what came off in such a wreck be his fault? And what if he was fast running out of money—it was the system at fault, not him! Zeke was losing his religion, turning Bolshevik.

Back there at Bahia Pulmo, he got on his high horse about the peasantry's liking for showing off their new cars—or guarding them—by parking on the beach. But now his better self had been compelled by unexpected circumstances to park where in jeopardy of onerously bogging down in legal sands—park in nothing so spiffy as a 4-wheel drive Toyota, either. His carcass just then, in fact, had been parked in a ramshackle old VW bus, like the cross-border visiting prole he was.

At the next town along, a uniformed officer of the law approached the driver. He straightened by the bus door. They had a little talk. About what?? A warm, arid dusk, and Zeke, there in the rear, was sweating with dread. A shiver ran up his spine.

About here, whenever Zeke aired this affair at a later date, he would interrupt his story to say like: "Believe me! I am not making this up for more suspense. It really happened. Just like that. The same as everything else I'm telling you.

Mexico: Trip 3

Travelers who fake the honest truth, who sneak in dramatic, made-up details and then pass off their accounts as what really happened to a trusting audience: little more than criminals!"

Okay. So there he was, sweating in terror, hot and bothered, cornered on a bus. An informer had seen him board at Mulege. Or maybe he was tailed to the bus by that courteous policeman who caught him in the act of removing baggage from his van and asked to what hotel he was going. At which Zeke hesitated, exactly as if his retention of hotel names in Spanish was as bad as it really was. Then stuttered, "Ah . . . Ah . . . Ah . . ." Then had to choose from among several which that obliging officer proceeded to guess in order to conclusively "remember." But was he only making up those names? Might that encounter have aroused suspicion? Did he call to verify?

The bus driver and the cop rattled on . . . and on . . . But with every eternal moment, their exchange grew less alarming. Hastily the driver reboarded, and the bus got away. Old drinking buddies or relatives—what a relief. Then there was less to fear until the next forenoon, when he got to the vicinity of the Tijuana jail and customs.

It gave him time to think about how he got where he was.

> What type is most liable to become a rover? Don't say "a mutt." Let's be scientific. Isn't it those puppies who have both above-average curiosity and more need of excitement than pleasure? Case in point, riding beastly buses like this one, in normal circumstances, yields more potentially harmful exposure and less creature comfort than staying put. Yet, these may well be part of a lifestyle that someone turns up and

elaborates in order to quit the boredom or strain of an overly familiar hometown.

Americans, cruising their interstate grooves, many commuting long distances to work, seem to have been taken over by travel. Although, a relatively simple and monotonous type, in private cars. Indeed, their smooth motoring has a hypnotic, dulling effect upon consciousness, if they're much like I was, before losing my automobile to a higher power.

Riding a public conveyance for lone, long-distance travel—what I'm doing now—is surely more inspirational to many than driving a car. It is so! The Secretary of Travel rides his chauffeured limousine; *he* doesn't drive. And remember, gulping down pavement in my own car, its radio on, more comfortably seated, over the long haul, too, racked up much annoyance and dissatisfaction— on top of more expense and risk of smash-up. Without some of the satisfying diversions that sometimes I have on a bus like this, either. Such as: undivided appreciation of good scenery, reading a superb paperback, music-listening on earphones, or (Developing) snickering at hilarious flaws in the crummy action flick on their overhead TV sets.

Tijuana

"Now my suspicion is that the universe is not only queerer than we suppose, but queerer than we can *suppose."* —Haldane, mathematical biologist.

Mexico: Trip 3

In the process of his long, drawn-out bus ride up the peninsula, Zeke realized that the day after next would be Easter Sunday—a major holiday weekend. Hoping for no one working police or immigration computers except bunnies with colored eggs, Zeke made up his mind to bide his time till Sunday to make his move. Unshaven, thin, and suspicious-looking, on Good Friday, Zeke did nothing better than check into a cheap hotel, the odor of old air conditioners and old cigars in his room.

Where, Saturday, as he lay on his back on the bedspread, mostly ignoring the ceiling and cobwebs above, he was wondering at the funny dogleg made by his fortunes of late. What had life done to him? By heeding the handwriting on the wall, he'd probably saved his neck there at Las Parras. That sudden recognition had then aggrandized his self-satisfaction almost to the extent of crediting divine intervention on his behalf. But then, the very next morning, an unaccountable accident, quick as lightning, ended his grand tour, claimed his car, put his liberty in peril. A strange conjunction of events if ever there was one! Should he take as gospel that the adage "Pride goeth before a fall" absolutely applies to anyone beginning to trust that Providence will all the time look out for him? Soon he would have to cross customs. If they ran his ID, had God now forsaken him?

There, to himself, he further reflected:
> It ain't necessarily so, but conceivably God takes a whole 'nother slant on faith than those gentlemen who wrote the Bible naturally assumed. It may actually prefer a certain amount of doubt as to Its reality among the general public. To that end, It has

Mexico: Trip 3

constructed a world that, superficially, seems meaningless. Thus, when It catches some living mortal peeking behind the scenes, It drops a sandbag on his noodle, figuratively speaking. (As a test of faith or a way of restoring a healthy skepticism?)

Its real mechanism for such corrective measures might involve blanking out a mortal's consciousness at precisely the right instant, thereby producing a costly enough mishap to persuade him or her that their life is not covered by any Transcendental Insurance policy after all.

As that may be, in Zeke's gray matter, God's anti-trust ray gun hit its target. What lasted of his faith was riddled with doubt again. Nonetheless, his belief in precognition, whatever that was, remained intact.

Zeke celebrated an agnostic's half-holiday that year by sitting on a bus in a dawdling line of buses, alongside a yet-longer queue of pedestrian atheists. The vast throng crept toward U.S. Customs (Judgment Day) at a snail's pace.

To kill time, he was entertaining the idea that the way to see Baja might be from a boat, rather than a car or bus. Stand far off from it, out at sea, as if it were a vast fresco on a wall. Baja needed distance! Thirsty landforms framed by blue sea and sky. It had more contrasting contour down along its shoreline, and more color. And for close viewing, there could be whales or other wildlife. Short expeditions inland from beaches would stumble upon unearthly flora and oases. All right, Baja needed distance!

Mexico: Trip 3

Eventually, it came his turn to expose himself to official scrutiny. Had there been a Mexican exit post, it went by so fast as to elude remembrance. Closed for the holiday, was it? Anyhow, the few U.S. inspectors not taking Easter off were swamped. A big day for tanned student carousers staggering back from spring break beyond the pale. It had every appearance of a big day for Mexicans going north of the border, too, though every day might be. All kinds of suspicious-looking characters were sneaking through immigration that day, Zeke reassured himself.

At the immigration point, our star made a special effort to keep his mouth relaxed and eyes steady, to act natural, and not wag his tail. He stepped up and awaited his doom. *Let's see,* thought the agent, *Big Bad Wolf has pointed upright ears, is heavyset, and also has longer, pointier fangs. So this must be Goofy.* One brief question, a glance at ID, and over he went. The end of Goofy's (aka Zeke's) last Baja roadtrip ever. Saved! Up in Disneyland.

Trip 4
(December 2003–January 2004)

Zeke set off for Central America via the southern part of Mexico, which he'd promised himself to see later, years earlier. After a Mexico City airport connection, Zeke landed in Huatulco. There was the only chance he'd have to skin dive for more than a month into his journey.

Huatulco

Playa La Entrega had white sand edged by a mixture of cactus and jungle. Only after passing up a snorkeling gear rental stand, it dawned upon Zeke how agreeable and easy floating on the surface would be with a lifejacket. It did when he came to the first strong, bubbly current off a rock pile. Where he trod water. After Santa Marta last trip, he was wary of Mexican beaches. Regardless, he continued on out. For *this* unusual beach had a safety rope with floats bounding its swimming area. **(41)**

Mexico: Trip 4

As for the bubbly rocks, Zeke had by then evolved a kind of balance skill at floating mostly face down while near shore rocks or coral. He was good at keeping space enough about his body through swells or low waves and crosscurrents. He'd gotten the feel of weightless, horizontal dancing in turbulent water while avoiding all cutting contact with nearby solids.

"Why did he snorkel?" First off, doubtless, many of the rewards from hiking, both aesthetic and physical, also applied. Then there was the fact that doing unusual outdoor sports, whether skin diving or skydiving, aided his make-believe tripping later on. Traces of recall made it easier to identify with, say, a character deep-sea scuba diving in a novel or film.

"Then why didn't he go in for scuba diving instead of skin diving? Rarely does entertainment feature snorkeling adventures." The reasons Zeke never bothered doing that were numerous: extra boat fares, equipment costs and procurement, required lessons. And, short of expertise at it, there was submitting to the scuba buddy system. Since Zeke liked hiking alone, he always presumed he'd go with strapping on his burdensome tanks and sinking into the deep to visit giant squid and sharks alone, too. Which sounded less carefree than either a lone walk in the woods or skin diving over reefs.

Huatulco had a splendid beach, but only fair coral. Arguably, the most beautiful part of the ocean is its coral reefs—fabulous colors and small, zippy, or placid sea creatures. It would seem that scuba diving promotes sighting *big* sea creatures. Notwithstanding, it was Zeke's experience that given long-enough persistence at it, amid select localities for it, one might also get their fill of sea life from skin diving. In as much as such denizens of the deep he eventually saw swim or crawl over various reefs embraced sea turtles, schools of big fish, things with tentacles, and even sharks. Or, for a yet-lower rate of adrenalin rush than snorkeling, there are aquariums of the first water.

Oaxaca

Out a main street from the *zocolo* about 1 a.m. marched a religious procession. Zeke looked on from a few stories up, on a roof. Skyrockets exploded over Oaxaca's highest structures. They were launched in the vicinity of the advancing procession; mostly for their booms, being devoid of lingering firework colors. While, just above street level, strings of crackers showered white sparks.

Two bands paraded. The first playing rapidly as possible, keeping up a frenzied cacophony, blown high-speed over a simple rhythm. With all the neighborhood dogs fervently barking dissonant counterpoint. Then came the second band, a few blocks behind, in charge of attacking a repetitious melody. Between them, big papier mâché figures were lifted. All of them depicting one busty woman: the city's patron saint. Her mobile heads went twisting this way and that, looming above two-story buildings, on the watch for sinners on any floor.

Surely, throwing firecrackers in itself is no sin. Which is why, in southern Mexico, innocent little boys could light and toss them, singly or in series, and not only on holy nights. One of the favorite toys thereabouts, they were, set off even in unlikely settings at odd hours. Whether on a quiet backstreet near a hotel at bedtime, in the lot of a national park during a shower, or in the air beside turning rear wheels of buses on a highway: BANG! ("Wrong, that wasn't a flat—keep going.")

Oaxaca—Monte Alban Ruins (!!!)—Oaxaca—Mitla Ruins (!!)—Yagul Ruins (!)

He was in a region of remote mystery-history, yet Zeke was beginning to feel that he'd seen more than enough Mesoamerican ruins for one lifetime. *Look at too many, and you no longer see them,* he was thinking. It was part of their mystique. Fortunately, next on his itinerary was one of the few national parks in southern Mexico without pre-Columbian ruins.

Tuxtla Gutierrez—Chiapa de Corzo—<u>Sumidero Canyon Nat. Pk.</u>

Off the boat, Zeke day-hiked the park. A big part of its excitement was due to the efforts of fancy, three-inch-long spiders, black with yellow leg bands and dots. Who insisted upon laying out their webs hither and yon across trails. Where they were almost impossible to spot every time. The same as any hiker would, though, Zeke always fought free. 'Twas always thus, but they never gave up on trying to capture him. Almost as bad, when nudged with a staff, these beauties would grab a hold and come chugging up toward his hand!

Beyond the big webs, there lay the round entrance to a deep shaft, which looked to have a horizontal cave or two radiating out from its bottom. Vines grew down its sides. He'd swear it was a *cenote!* Yet Zeke wasn't Tarzan-enough to trust all those little vines with his weight all the way down. Then, too, he may have been out of spare batteries or something. So he left there with no good reason to thump his chest and bellow. Although he could just imagine how fine that would have echoed up from the bottom.

Overhead, many vultures with white tails and wingtips soared above the canyon, both in small flocks and large gyres. Big birds, deep holes, spiders: all his trail needed was canyon-edge vistas. But its yellowish sides were hidden at every turn by viney, low trees or higher-elevation bamboo.

Temperate-zone trails more often make for better walks than tropical ones, even omitting hot-and-humid tropical climate. Because, what they do have is more interesting middle-distance visibility of canyon sides, hillsides, meadows, boulders, etc. They tend to show more; their vegetation being less-often dense and close than along tropical trails.

One sort of low tree had yellow, fleshy blossoms, and many birds among small fruit pods, with airy sky-puzzles in its scant crowns, and many blossoms intact on the ground below, not wilted. Their mild, sweet scent was in the air. As were bright orange butterflies with long, rather narrow, bird-like wings. Also, midsize butterfly conformists in black with day-glow orange tail stripes—got up to resemble spiders. Or were the spiders imitating *them*?

Twenty-foot cacti and big agave with curling maroon tips were numerous. Trees with big, cone-shaped thorns up their trunks, there were, too, and coppery, peeling, paper-barked trees, like on Baja. There came the harsh, scolding cry of a sizable bird hiding in bamboo: a parrot?

Villahermosa—Palenque

In a patch of jungle near town, Zeke slept in a poorly screened, thatched-roof *palpa*. Next morning, as he rolled his sleeping bag, a medium-sized non-venomous black spider rushed out and away. Which accounted for both the numerous bite marks on his delicious flesh and why he wasn't poisoned. A tarantula. Although they weren't properly introduced until later, in Guatemala, by a jungle guide at El Zotz ruins. Where that spider and many others lurked in the fallen leaves by the edge of the campground, some two or three inches in length and width. Their many eyes glowed in his flashlight beam. Thereafter, at Tikel ruins, one who looked like the spider he met at Palenque scurried into the dorm from the hotel garden when he opened the door, and Zeke exacted his revenge. Stomped him! **(42)**

Palenque Ruins

What a drag to show up less than an hour after opening yet see and hear get-togethers atop most temple platforms and about their bases. A seated lady, when he first walked into the central plaza, gave him a smug, superior smile as if to declare unbeatable touristic skill and timing. In any event, the jungle environing was as compelling an element in their beauty as the ruins themselves. Broad-leaved trees of many species with big-leaved vines hanging all over. Unexcavated ruins down a path with Mayan stone paving past a small waterfall were more enchanting than the main temple area. Likewise, some by a trail beyond them were, with those fluttering orange butterflies again. **(43)**

Ancient Palenque had about four residents per square meter. Some Mayan researchers blame population density that high with undermining the local dynasty. No matter why, the city was abandoned only about 150 years after it was built. It couldn't have been too many tourists back then—too many arthropods?

Palenque
"Buses depart for San Javier, near Bonampak, every three hours," he read. But there were about three bus "stations" in the town, probably consisting of one to three vehicles each, parked on obscure side streets. Therewith, poor old Zeke was confronted by a considerable inconvenience. So he mentally shrugged and went in for a cheaper and handier *collectivo*.

"Why mention that?" a green *gringo* might wonder.

"As a warning, señor."

Zeke's cramped spot on the van's hard seat, over by the window, was much higher than its sagging middle. Therefore, the whole sixty-mile trip, his butt fought gravity. From self-defense against it, he suffered a leg complaint—enough soreness for a bout of limping upon arrival. **(44)**

San Javier—Bonampak Ruins and Biological Reserve
They wanted $7 to ride a park bus from the edge of the reserve in to the ruins! From roadside before a trail sign that said: "*Zona arqueologica 3 horos.*" Thrifty as always, Zeke decided to walk it next morning. He camped around the first bend from the gate in dense cover.

Mexico: Trip 4

There were occasional loud and elaborate tropical birdcalls, but his first twilight there featured a continuing background swell, rising and then falling, from a breathy growl to a low sizzle. Every so often, it paused. Then a couple dogs would take their turn barking before the mystery noise came on again. What it sounded like was an infernal machine in some farmyard, turned on all night to scare away wild animals and campers—but that wasn't plausible. Who could have guessed: monkey choir practice!

Next day, on the trail, Zeke kept going where he should have turned off. But the trail sign was buried under a fallen tree dense with big-eared jungle vines, and, when he found his way back to it, he could see another blow-down beyond. Then, still farther back, he took a new trail that, in six hours or so, fortunately, led him to the dirt road about 1 km. from the park gate and his hidden gear at dusk. True, the only ruins he saw that day were those of huge uprooted trees. Yet, 'twas a creative failure, he afterwards thought. Since the jungle again proved as spectacular as the ruins it hid. **(45)**

He got to them next morning. Post-ruins, he broke camp and backpacked a short way in search of a quieter campsite. Quiet being a major issue with jungle camping, what with the cries of night birds and the sounds of animals tromping by. While in contrast, visual *privacy*, not far off trail, was almost too absolute for safety. Thus, after twenty paces into a gloomy penetrability through the foliage, after looking down some to hunt levelness, upon looking up and about, then turning his eyes and frame once around, there came over him a hint of panic. Attached to the question of how lost he was just then.

Mexico: Trip 4

Compass in hand, he endured a few anxious moments. After which our Zeke only managed to merge with his damn trail a good ways from right where he'd put his pack earlier. The one with his canteen, tent, and other survival gear in it. These were bad moments, during which he slipped into an inner space of feeling half-or-more *"Lost!"* While he skeptically heeded his instrument's questionable advice. Jungle bushwhacking was like trying to navigate a ship in a thick, green Irish fog, but with bouncing off an iceberg less probable than treading too near a snake. **(46)(47)**

That black night, he was awakened by one or more large animals browsing among leaves near his tent. Could they be agoutis, or even capybaras? (Giant jungle rodents.) . . . The thought of big cats held his interest, too. And the "infernal machine" growled on as he slept. Nearly as absorbing as that patch of forest was for losing oneself in fancies or nightmares was its ruined city. Where did the Maya empire go? Were they lost and eaten by their genes? Their pool giving rise to a male population with too many rats and too few mice, resulting in too much spilled blood, both in their overabundant wars and religious sacrifices?

Their ruin had faded cartoon murals and eroded bas-reliefs on stone slab stelae, which were not unlike high, rectangular North American tombstones in shape. The toons portrayed its former male citizens as barrel-chested and stocky with short necks. Moreover, they had fat legs with splayed feet. (Or craftsmen who drew legs badly?) Their faces had prominent noses—long, high-bridged, sometimes hooked—with protruding Asian mouths and lips to reinforce the bigness of

Mexico: Trip 4

their honkers. Narrow, angry-looking eyes. Reddish-brown skin. Zeke was glad they so much lost their way in the jungle as to never find him.

The main step pyramid on the Gran Plaza had one long staircase up to a high platform. With treads so shallow that Zeke's toes had to be turned outward slightly—both to go up and for his precarious, slow descent. Splayed! More than as a warlord's sacred tomb—which it also was—it may have been designed as a sort of defensive artificial hill-of-last-recourse for foot soldiers, near the center of their flat territory. A vantage point from which to rain down spears and such upon an enemy whom the force of gravity kept from throwing much back with accuracy, especially while running or crawling upward, exposed upon very uneven and scant footing.

They may have gotten some of their military architectural concepts from their indigenous ants. Which built *their* hills about 3-ft. (1 m.) high, with a 15-ft. (180 m.) by 5-ft. (1½ m.) base. Approaching which, across jungle footpaths, there trickled long, wiggly lines of green leaf bits, their bearers underneath barely visible in the dim light. Leaf-cutter ants streaming all day in the shadow of huge trees with their buttress roots and connecting vines.

Elsewhere, across the trail marched columns of army ants: 10 yards (1 m.) or so wide, of unknown length. Formidable as any species of ant gets—best waded in boots. Zeke jogged across. In the instants when his heels and soles touched ground, many red ants boarded his feet, crossed his sock tops, and sprinted up his legs, only pausing to bite. With any luck, in picking them off, he'd also find a few ticks. **(48)**

Mexico: Trip 4

Frontera Corozal (Echeverra)—Rio Usumacinta and Yaxchilam Ruins

His boat went downstream on a fast jungle river. Four or more tan sandstone steps paralleled its course; neat erosion, seen between greenery. Occasional reptiles and birds stood, sat, or lay upon these sand bleachers. Broken human remnants rose on a high peninsula beneath which the water made a U-turn.

Tall stone-step platforms with sundry stone temples and other constructions on top. Some of the higher had massive walls up there. One platform temple, the weirdest, had its decorative roof crest intact. Below which lay a long rectangular honeycomb with lines of square windows—looking like a dormitory of five low-ceiling floors. A smaller pyramid had big stucco masks of Kin, the Sun. Then there were bas-reliefs showing the Vision of the Snake self-sacrifice rituals. While off the Gran Plaza was a ball court with more ritual significance: members of the losing team were sacrificed. Any excuse for ritual suicide or murder—didn't they like the jungle?

The site and river, as at Bonampak, had howler monkeys making their far-off beastly roar. Much closer were a gang of Mexican children bawling "Mama!" at the top of their lungs for almost fifteen minutes, repeatedly, without pause. Incited by howler monkeys! Nonetheless, way up and over a few root-covered flights of stone stairs was solitude in the Temple of the Sun. Although there the monkeys, themselves, were sounding shorter-range, louder, and were accompanied by some bat squeaks. At nightfall, the jungle turned black and heavy, like a temple.

Palenque—Misol-ha waterfalls

The best out of three watery stopping places for tour buses. 115-ft. (35 m.) falls into a lush tropical pool, it was. Near its foot, and then near the next two rushing tourist scenes, overdevelopment, though no more overcrowded than was to be expected. Seeing that water is the most popular object in nature for humans on vacation to sense. At Misol-ha, busloads channeled onto narrow rock pathways, which stepped up their speed of flow, to out where they spouted or gushed from their viewing platform.

Cascadas Agua Azul

At Agua Azul, more pressing and gushing; although most of it in the parking area. Zeke was coming down with water on the brain:

> Of all varieties of natural beauty, rapidly moving water has the widest appeal. All beauty, artificial or not, has certain particular elements which attract the notice of nearly everyone. Well, graceful motion is to vision as rhythm is to listening. It being the most widely noticed aspect of one kind of sensual beauty. A kind which resides mostly in nature (fountains excepted), not music.
>
> Adding to the charm of waterfalls or cascades are their relative novelty. Of novelty in all forms, energetic motion and loud sound are where things get most interesting for most. Hence the terrific attraction of crashing, powerfully moving water

that also shifts from its normal color to white, as gaseous mist explodes from its base, within a compact field of vision. Whereas, a beach with offshore whitecaps does not seriously rival a high waterfall, if only because the sea is too big. Which makes most of its waviness too commonplace. Beauty but less novelty it commonly has, except at a relatively few select locations or times.

Agua Clara Nature Reserve

Here they aimlessly crossed and then re-crossed a suspension bridge, Zeke included. Who was masquerading as a high-and-mighty tourist that day, transportation schedules and fares being what they were going south.

San Cristobal de las Casas—Laguinos de Montebello Nat. Pk.

Its pine-and-oak temperate forest at the lakes changed to tropical rainforest at higher elevation. The lakes showed a variety of vivid blue to green hues. North of the campground were some caves and a river through a natural arch, with mineral-dyed shades of white, pink, gray, and ocher near their entrances. Inside, masses of joined stalactites were hanging like udders. A patch of collapsed cave roof had big vines draping. Most of the stalagmites under a foot thick were stolen. Some of the stalactites were broken and gone, too. Yet more survived here than did in a larger cave he'd seen at San Cristobal.

Through a hole in a corner of the cave, an underground stream ran into a green reflecting pool at its mouth. Up from

Mexico: Trip 4

one side of which rose a scramble of about 20 ft. into an upper low-roofed cave with smaller stalactites still intact. At its rear, through a wide crack, dangled green plants. Also there was a hole filled with daylight, through which Zeke climbed out. Grutas San Rafael del Arco may well have been the most fascinating cave that he ever entered. Then later, at dusk, came one of the loveliest birdcalls he'd ever heard—lengthy and melodic.

"You want us to believe you experienced those two things on the same day in the very same park?" a skeptic once asked.

To which Zeke shot back: "Would I lie about anything that important?" Said with such conviction that anyone would have to believe him.

Caverns are to minerals what waterfalls are to water. It's where they put on their most popular display, once made easy of access; they become overcrowded geological freak shows, with their stalactites and so on. In the U.S., these use overstated ads to pull in tons of underground groupies at stupendous ticket prices. But not necessarily so in good old Mexico, way out on a park road.

Mostly, well-advertised caverns no longer seemed worth it to Zeke. They weren't even as conducive to thought as walking into a cinema might be. Not while moving right along and listening to everybody noisily near on their narrow walkways. What's more, in Third World caves, all the stalactites getable by ladder were liable to be as missing or damaged as their stalagmites.

The next day didn't go so well. Zeke set out backpacking eastward for some of the more celebrated lakes, in early morning, with little campground traffic yet. But he soon found himself tromping pavement where his map showed a softer dirt road. Mostly uphill 4 1/2 miles with heavy, fast, and close traffic swooshing by. A trudge only interrupted, partway to La Canada lakes, by walking a short off-road track.

To Lago Montebello: polluted with at least detergent, though with a couple white herons at the far end. Its wilderness feel long gone; its carrying capacity exceeded. Merchants in stalls by the road, trash from these and motorists accumulating, deep tire tracks in the mud at shoreline. Still, in sunlight, the water held two shades of blue. While farther La Canada lake, almost cut in two by rocky outcrops, extended its colors from tangerine to pastel green in its shallows over yellowish rocks and mud. Brimming craters below cliffs or steep hills, navy blue in deeper water, unpolluted from relative inaccessibility.

Most of the other small lakes were also inaccessible. Was it more to preserve them from the Indian park dwellers or the roadsters? Anyway, on the highway, there were *collectivos*, and even occasional buses whizzed by. Or Zeke might have hitched, had he known soon enough that the first lake he actually wanted was over two miles and worth the wait. **(49)**

Chinkultic ruins

They were close to the park, but no path went there. Trees full of bromeliads, Spanish moss, and ferns grew roundabout the main remains, which were covered in vegetation. Also, there stood a high temple overlooking, from a tan-white cliff, a sinkhole and system of lakes, the one nigh pale green. Vultures soaring. White herons. An eagle to the east. Blue

Mexico: Trip 4

and pink morning glories. Tall yellow daisies and other pink wildflowers. The most beautiful landscape surrounding any Maya ruin seen in Mexico by Zeke.

Huehuetenango, Guatemala

Zeke then crossed the Guatemala border. The first city he came to that day was Huehuetenango (not: Who? Who can tango?). He stopped before sundown and went into a small hotel. At the desk, a pretty Indian woman was holding her baby. Great, as the first thing he wanted to know was if someone there did laundry, the price of that. She held up four fingers. By which Zeke misunderstood her to be asking ten times what she really meant. He made a lower offer. She chuckled, asked another woman in another room, refused his bid, and only then wrote hers out, to which Zeke immediately agreed. Obviously, she was new at her job and unused to foreigners. Haggling the rent went faster.

Next day, sheets hanging to dry were ducked by Zeke in descending from his attic room on a wide-stepped ladder with railings. Then, on the second floor, through an open window, he caught sight of most of his own laundry laid out to dry on a gently sloping tin roof. Almost dry, too—just beginning to blow off in the light breeze. A shirt slid over the ridge and down the far side aways as he looked.

Zeke trod cautiously out, grabbed an armful of the larger pieces, climbed to his room, came back with a stuff sack, and purposefully strode (tango-style) out to get the rest. A few steps and—CRUNCH!—he fell right through the roof!

Mexico: Trip 4

Only about up to his chest, though. His left boot's toe having struck a crossbeam below, while his left arm he flung by reflex over the roof ridge to his side. Otherwise, he would have fallen one story into a tiled hallway and maybe broken a foot or leg. A near-miss disaster! All because, unfortunately, that time out, he'd stepped on and through a roofing strip that, in place of tin, was a same-color plastic fiberboard—no stronger than cardboard. Watch out for those Guatemalan roof traps! **(50)**

After this freak accident, bad recollections of assorted Mexican hotels and so forth descended. Could Central America be worse? Should he quit his journey to Panama, fraught with hardship and peril, before it was too late?

Only his lust for adventure (in clean clothes) drove him onward. Despite the fact that about ¾ of the hotels that he could afford in the southern provinces of Mexico had either a barking dog or a crowing rooster in a yard or alley right beside them. While restaurants almost invariably had loud TVs or stereos. That or the din and fumes of an adjacent highway or busy street by their open front or windows. Plus the fact that more than half the hotel rooms had mosquitoes buzzing after dark.

Light-sleeping Zeke wasn't used to it. For in North American cities, what he mostly got instead of pets or livestock resounding were sirens of emergency vehicles, car alarms, trucks beeping loud as they backed, boys broadcasting high-volume gangsta rap, and the garbage men of dawn. Then, in the suburbs all day long: power lawn mowers or hedge trimmers, motorcycles, helicopters, and leaf blowers impinged upon distractible Zeke. Talk about bad vibes! Reducing these sources of stress wasn't a negligible motive for travel abroad.

Almost any way but south would have improved things. The best technique for the deeper south, he decided, was to carry and mostly sleep in a tent with perfect mosquito netting. Commonly lodging in cities only long enough to buy supplies, shower, and do his wash. Otherwise, camping mostly in the howling wilderness parks. . . . By so doing, he made it to Panama.

EPILOGUE

From Panama, he flew home again, back to the same old grind. There to take possessions out of storage, rent a room, and find a temporary clerical job. Wherever he underwent it, in whatever season, he was accustomed to frown on the static part of his subsistence.

"What am I doing *here* again, in *City X!?*"

"Still putting up with my usual incompetence," was the answer. Some fresh mistake would often be his lead-in to reminiscence and a clarification of why he was where he was.

For quite a while, since darkest adolescence, in lucid intervals after assorted humiliations and letdowns, Zeke had been musing that he should withdraw from public. Since they found it so easy to look down on him, he should keep strictly away from them. Although, at first, he wanted to presume that his interactive failures were the product of too little effort rather than lack of ability. That he had the wrong temperament and physique for the job. Or, as he later came to see it, from being

Epilogue

so untalented at playing guinea pig as to make the exertion futile.

What basically kept his withdrawal conception from leading to action in his teens was propaganda for adjustment or growth through involvement—coming from parents, school, books, movies, TV, and the rest. Although, doubtless, there was also economic dependence on his father, casual kind words from well-wishers, and the inertia of hometown convention to keep him in check. So he kept isolated while reading and reading, but that was about as far as he went.

Then, away at college, a mildly positive illusion about his career prospects dried up. Some dorm-living out there, and it sank in that his melancholic, mousy demeanor would not get him far anywhere in the adult world, academia included. This judgment added to his variable depression.

Due to his solitary nature, he shied away from clubs, ball games, horse races, and any other opportunities for useful contacts at his Midwestern university. Trying to memorize what might be on the next test while putting up with dormitory distractions removed any temptation for the extracurricular. Professors, too, next to never saw him out of their lecture halls, if there. He'd always be a good ways off, at the gallop on tracks and fields far removed. So when they laid their bets on who might run first in *their* field, Zeke hadn't the gait of an easy winner. Not the pony to bet on, he drew poor odds.

His grades implied his retention of what teachers were orally emphasizing was, at best, average. He much preferred reading. Lectures made his mind wander. So that his unreliable near-term recall of verbalized facts and phrases kept him

Epilogue

on the bench, with losing scores all season. But Zeke wasn't beaten yet! To get even for bad calls in a few required meets, he began cutting them. Then, exercising on his own, he lapsed back into his bad high school study habit of cracking unassigned classics. At which little game, though he was hitting homers way out of his teachers' fields, he didn't qualify for an athletic scholarship. Then, it only took one San Francisco summer, a few good scores there, a couple more truly despicable ones back in Iowa, and he quit the team.

Soon thereafter, he was hitchhiking in southeastern Arizona, back to the west coast, and got a ride going all the way to Palm Springs, California. With Eli, an articulate mouse his own age, who took an indirect route through the mountains, as they both liked scenic viewpoints. Sort of a travel affinity developed between them, in fact. Then the elevation near Bisbee gave Eli's dated Oldsmobile the hiccups. It threatened to stall. But despite its carburetor, they finally made it. (What a coincidence it was that both Elijah and Ezekiel had first names of Hebrew prophets that began with E, though one was using an alias.)

In Palm Springs, they pulled up before a glassy, split-level desert dwelling, well landscaped. Stepping out of Eli's clunker, Zeke breathed in the cool of the town's aromatic twilight, the jasmine. And he liked where he was. Definitely he did after Eli enlightened him that, though all the residents therein preferred seeing themselves as family, they were not genuine kin. That, in fact, a live-in Gestalt therapy group was what they all knew underneath was going on—Cedu.

Epilogue

A small-scale offshoot of Synanon, which was based in Santa Monica—at first a highly successful drug-rehabilitation foundation. Until its director, Dederick, mad with power, declared it a religion, chiefly for tax purposes. After which a secret inner circle of unregenerate rats made it into a front and recruiting office for various criminal activities, the least being tax evasion. It had to disband in 1989.

Cedu wasn't for "dopers" so much as boys and girls with "character disorders." There were three adults and about twelve young, disorderly characters in residence. After only a few of their encounter sessions, Zeke was invited to stay on. Their being convinced by then that he was goofy, though not addicted *yet*—only in distress, in his own quiet way. Well, lucky for him, the group's guiding principle was that, by strengthening their expressions of feeling, in their daily "games," its members would learn to get along okay in the outside world. While another aspect of their quest, scarcely mentioned, was reform of their undesirable behaviors through peer pressure.

Lounging upon an oval of padded furniture while raising a hue and cry against others or defending oneself, the louder the better—that was how their game went. And to a mouse on the receiving end, it was like sitting on a court witness stand daily before a team of wacky prosecuting attorneys who derived real pleasure from slamming, tearing to shreds, and ridiculing his testimony, attributes, and each of his trifling misbehaviors. Scornful laughter and gibes were the bulk of what he got and gave most sessions. Some, in faking or venting feelings of aggravation or frustration, also liked to yell. Out to extract or imitate a "gut-level response," they were. While only a few, Zeke among them, excelled at finding fault with incoming accusations and then fending them off with humor. Or else covering themselves with excuses in a rational tone.

His reserve was deplored, and often denounced. It was fortunate for him, they felt, that he was getting the unrelenting attention that incited nuts of his ilk to crack. To loosen up and act out or, where feasible, let it all hang out—just like most there. Who would sure enough crack up derisively at *others* then under indictment with minimal justification. Inasmuch as the tribe was accustomed to that, not some mannerly mold of pagan rite—therapeutic for anger-management issues—where the medicine man or woman intones "I'm glad you shared that with us," like in kindergarten. Nevertheless, it took an awful lot to make Zeke holler! Even at kindergarten teachers! That was just the way he felt—or rather didn't so much.

The chief—a know-it-all psychiatrist, name of Mel—maintained that, if he put up with it long enough, he would "grow"—bring forth an improved self. Still and all, regarding growth-speak, Zeke was skeptical, or grew to be. Soaking up how one is seen by a roomful of confidants is one thing, but making a constructive change in one's temperament and childhood influences is quite another, he came to feel. To such an extent that, later in life, he lost all conviction in the growth potential of losing it loud-voiced, imitation or otherwise. And even grew into the opinion that such a game might be to contemporary psychotherapy about what snake oil was to obsolete medical treatment.

Yet he hung on in Palm Springs for months, and chipped in on the rent through a couple monotonous jobs. So what

Epilogue

was the particulate density of his situation, to make him settle in so long, inhaling jasmine on the way home? Early twenties he was then. With age, later, it was an uphill effort remembering more than the jasmine and the first names of a few confidants there.

A rough biographer's guess at why he put up with daily ridicule so long? From Zeke's reckoning that fervent confrontations were a fast way of getting to know thyself. For his private assessments of his socializing abilities were often distorted by temporary optimism. Or else his deep-think on the matter was invaded by vain schemes for self-improvement. Rather, he wanted the truth about how differing spectators saw him, after confessing this and that, presuming that some of their views would be more accurate than what he could see on his own. Which might, in the process, encourage him to shake off some of his shyness and make friends, since hitchhiking had, in a more concrete context.

In a marathon session, up for most of the night, brainwashed with a little help from his friends—selected Beatles tunes during breaks—Zeke had an identifiable "peak experience." In which the others and then he caught him moving and talking while observing himself less: acting more self-expressively than average, involuntary emotions showing. While he was absolutely sober! Amidst considerable chaste hugging and sheer joy, felt and released in a group setting. While feeling deeply that everyone there approved of him as a well-meaning "family" member and therefore accepted what all he said and did. (Within reason. Although, theoretically,

Epilogue

"unconditional love" was in the air.) It was the greatest party of his life—not that he ever got invited to many.

The following sessions were back to business as usual, though the gang's rhetoric was boldly less inhibited, and now their focus was squarely upon *him*. After he opened up like that in surfing his peak, they smelled blood in the water. Their indictments of him, as usual, mostly homed in on his ingrained anti-authoritarianism and immaturity, but now with more emphasis. Even so, the former bad trait, Zeke felt that he could easily live with. After all, according to what he acquired in college from bumper stickers, to "Question Authority" was a duty due a slogan boost or boast. When, however, the gang caught on that they couldn't worry him much with that one, they began to walk in lockstep behind their top dog in coming down hard on his immaturity.

The menace of chronic immaturity, in those days, undeniably bothered Zeke. He was practically a virgin, for one thing. For his baby face and slimness, topped off with a seriously timid bearing, were outrageously off-putting to women. This was before he knew by heart that he was a mouse, and before the word "nerd" was even invented. Moreover, his politeness was not what it should have been, either. Causing a sympathetic man who once gave him a ride to marvel to his father how "naïve" he was for his age. Part of a tactfully obscure telephone warning against his gadding about. (Mel, after Freud, diagnosed his roaming as a search for somebody of importance gone missing—his mother, who died when he was four.)

Epilogue

There was one particular that his team of prosecuting attorneys even then didn't know about him, though. Notwithstanding that he may have let them in on it once or twice. That being how long his inmost mind lingered and suffered over criticism, whether from self or outsourced. Especially that aimed at his ego's softest spots and his worst behavior. Case in point: while driving the house car, he came close to a bad traffic accident. All his fault: wrong way on a one-way street. Now that, in hindsight, *did* make him look obviously immature. (Or was it asking to have his diaper changed at a service station afterwards?) His essential, longer-lasting plight was low self-esteem, though.

After the marathon, beneath Mel's and everyone's daily, redundant spankings over his immaturity, Zeke—oh so gradually—felt his horrible, suppressed wrath turn outward. Predominantly at one witty authority whose program he questioned, but whose critical notice he nevertheless dreaded—Mel. "*Down* with him!" But then, rather than loudly make the big stink everybody awaited or, unrelieved, offer up his bawls, he dropped out of the "family." (Although partially, his departure was also due to a relapsing nomadic itch, like diaper rash.)

Zeke left the security of his Palm Springs oasis and receded into the impersonal desert of southern California. While in the distance, his new, confident identity wavered and dissolved, like a mirage, or like San Bernardino on a smoggy day. Although he at first felt more likable, less alienated, more poised, that lasted only a few days. Then he came down. His self-esteem sank to about where it was before.

Epilogue

There was nothing to be done. Without a girlfriend or role in life, drifting, he had no continuing contact with anyone. And it slipped his mind what he'd imbibed at the university dorm about social-mindedness being facilitated by vodka. Besides, of late he'd been led to believe, on the evidence of his encounters at Palm Springs, that self-confidence was necessarily sparked by time spent confessing innermost thoughts and feelings to others. Letting them stream out without manipulation—without falsification, censorship, or reordering—that was the way to do it. Thinking aloud: trusting words out of your mouth straight to at least one ear willing and able to appreciate them.

Doing transient restaurant chores, while groping for his missing knack of frank talk with familiars, his forced banter with waitresses or anybody often sounded pretentious. As if he couldn't adjust to a lower level of discourse. Telling topics were never introduced or were left dangling. Commonplace remarks he would make with unnecessarily dramatic emphasis, his intonation out of alignment with their import. Or else he might stretch for some bit of wit that just exceeded his grasp. After his Gestalt therapy self-assurance and candor trickled away, left was only a cautious residue of adult thought-control. To skirt the tedium of which ran Zeke's tried-and-true rut of reserve.

Not that there was often enough leeway or peace for idle chat at a job. Having a solid meeting of minds with ease and all-embracing participation seemed to require an artificial arrangement. With unbroken expanses of time set aside and a pacesetter there to lead the pack and keep the gab flowing. But even with all that in place, as Zeke learned, any poise

Epilogue

sprouting from such interludes of openness and charm could be stored for only a short while, once away from the ongoing party. About as long as leftovers in the refrigerator could.

Soon, getting up steam on his own, Zeke was not even meeting, let alone hanging out with and charming anyone. Partly from his being mistrustful of rewards from sociability. For when he sorted them out, it seemed that most of his clumsiest disasters—outcomes of regrettably bad decisions or indecisions—sprang from being pressured by someone intimate. While his happier life involved no more than interactions with strangers or passing acquaintances—left behind after only a few conversations, before they could affect his plans. Those were his times relatively free of occasions for sorrow and major regret, with periods of hiking his most trouble-free of all.

At an early age, he realized his susceptibility to allowing his druthers to be overridden by someone's demands to whom he felt close. That his own way of doing things, in fool control, uninfluenced by others, ordinarily came out better. Self-knowledge that he sometimes forgot. At which times there came over him the vain wish to make friends, especially a girlfriend, if only for sexual experience. Inasmuch as they or she, as confidants, might build his confidence and rid him of mousiness. Buddies the foothills and girls the summit path to self-esteem it seemed to a boy with only fair-to-middling sex drive for the climb. Whereas, what he didn't suspect until much later was that reserve might be an essential demonstration of his innermost, stubborn-most mental climate. Rather than only some kind of oversensitive, neurotic insecurity that he should outgrow.

Epilogue

Also much later, Zeke became cognizant of a definite pattern to his longer friendships and few love affairs. That at some near interval, there arose a practical case for him to go his separate way rather than go on in another's presence—some difficult situation. Then that's what he did—escape, evade, avoid. Leave town rather than persist long enough for any stable connection, he would. A rambler: one with little instinct to keep track of those whom he got to know and then left behind.

Any who weren't as insistent about mail and visitation as his father, at any rate. One with a family claim on him, it would have to be. Zeke could have made someone a very faithful husband, whether home with her or away on another continent. Perhaps leaving potential friends or lovers was an old, subconscious behavior pattern from when, at four, his mother left. At an age he didn't know that her death was involuntary. (In one of his few, doubtful memories of her: "Learn to amuse yourself," she said.)

During his sojourn in Riverside, Zeke read two volumes of *The Lord of the Rings*, an allegorical masterpiece. Its thinly disguised theme being that humankind must defeat the many totalitarian rat armies and their other organizations, and thereby destroy the use of coercion and violence in biped affairs. Volumes in which "hobbits" represent mice, while the other members of Frodo's Fellowship are guinea pigs. These represented by an assortment of fabulous critters—elves, dwarfs, humans. The plot centers on a long quest by a hobbit and his allies for a specific volcano in which to melt a black-magic ring.

Epilogue

This level of subtext is overlaid by a medieval nostalgia account of honorable knights and royalty fighting and mostly winning to defend territory against evil wizard megalomaniacs and their overwhelming hosts of subhuman monsters. Antique military clashes with much ennoblement of antique military virtues. A cleaned-up recollection of Western civilization's sword-fighting glory days. (Or gory days.) The Dark Ages transmuted from history into myth.

Books that brought tears to Zeke's eyes. Which no fiction had accomplished since a Dostoevsky novel in early adolescence. And part of why they did was equating his Gestalt group, recently quit, with the land of the elves. Reinforcing that was the depiction of a saintly crusade, merging adventures afoot with loyal male companions, beautiful women, and virtue. Encouraging Zeke's youthful sensibility that such, for him, was within the realm of possibility, as well as desirable. Along with the wishful parallel thought that errantry advances maturing. (For, at his homecoming, Frodo's old village neighbors declare that his journey has transformed him, so he can now well handle all his own affairs.)

From this source, which some might call silly, Zeke derived a glimmering goal or reinforced tilt, quixotic even, in the direction of hitting trails abroad. With the result that he tried his first hikes in a foreign country. One with plenty of volcanoes. Mexico.

APPENDIX
ZEKE'S GUIDE TO TRAVEL AND LIFE:
problems & solutions

1. Problem: Exactly how to find the best seat on a train. Solution: After finding out for sure the train at hand is the right one, with no reserved seats and a big crowd surging toward it, walk quickly to the farthest car of your class from the station. There, try for the quietest window seat on the best side for scenery, according to your map estimate. Try for one facing the train front, and not facing other seats. (Developing) In hot regions, walk through several cars before choosing a seat. Notice whether the temperature increases or decreases in some direction (due to faulty air conditioning). Make temperature and the density of noisy adults, children, or babies the criteria for choosing a car.

2. Problem: What time to arrive at a station or port when you happen to know only one scheduled departure time for a vehicle and don't have a phone or the native language.

Appendix

Solution: When the next departure time of a public conveyance is known, but subsequent departure times are uncertain, and with no convenient way to learn them, try to be ready one hour before the sure time. Do not put off leaving someplace with only a rough notion of its public-conveyance schedule.

3. Problem: How to avoid missing land-transportation departures. Solution: The evening before taking a long-distance land vehicle with infrequent departures, figure what time to awaken. Allow 2 hours to shower and pack (2½ camping or to take advantage of a hostel bed-and-breakfast deal). Add ½ hour transit time to reach the place of departure. Then add the delay-proofing, pre-departure times below (in "4") to that figure, according to type of public conveyance. Subtract that sum from the departure time. Then set your alarm, if you might be asleep then. Or else make a note of the very latest to start for the terminal. (Exception: To reach a distant airport or an overland station in the suburbs from a big city center, or coming downtown to one from the suburbs, add 1 hour transit time instead of ½ hour.) [This formula may vary for different individuals with different morning routines.]

4. Problem: How long should be reserved for pre-departure delays while at land-transportation stations? Solution: (Modern) Reach train and bus stations at least ½ hour before departure time. Also reach outdoor bus stops or shelters at least ½ hour before the boarding time of one that makes infrequent runs. (Developing) Reach train and bus stations at least 1 hour

Appendix

before departure time in countries where they often leave early or late—otherwise, ½ hour before.

5. Problem: How to deal with rats. **Solution:** Do not accompany a rat anywhere. Avoid developing an acquaintanceship with any. And be especially careful not to enter the private car of a probable rat. But if, in some situation, doing so seems worth the risk, secretly note their license plate number.

6. Problem: How to deal with boozers. **Solution:** (Developing) Treat drinkers respectfully, but never accept invitations to join them. Being in a hurry, however, is not a good enough excuse. Tell them that alcohol causes you severe headaches or something. [Once you agree, leaving them soon is apt to cause greater offense than immediate refusal.]

7. Problem: What about hitching a ride on a bus, where they may stop if signaled? **Solution:** (Developing) While hitching anywhere outside a city, try signaling buses going your way. Should one stop, notice its destination sign before boarding, to recite it if asked by the driver. Exit, however, soon after it turns off your planned route. (Exception: Where a short bus ride is likely to result in worse hitchhiking.)

8. Problem: How to behave with a likely rat on a remote path. **Solution:** (Developing) Alone on foot in wilderness or countryside, if you encounter a probable rat, be polite, and keep talking. With lots of smiling and plentiful eye contact. Act

Appendix

pleased to meet him. Language permitting, ask his name and hometown. [Rats may be more likely to attack if they detect fear or dislike. Many are nearly blind to pretense, however.]

9. Problem: What equipment to carry for rat control. Solution: (Developing) Walk no trails alone without tear gas. If it goes lost, broken, or empty, unless it can be replaced, omit further off-road hikes during the trip. Omit risky urban areas, too, in countries with high crime rates. And consider whether to shop for another weapon somewhere abroad or return home immediately.

10. Problem: When are churches open? Solution: When a Roman Catholic church interior is on your itinerary, best try visiting early in the morning (7 or 8 a.m.–9 or 10 a.m.). For an Orthodox Eastern church, Sunday about 9 a.m.–noon may be best. For Protestant churches, ask their open hours. But going to any kind, for better lighting, avoid going after dark. [Many in large cities remain open for long periods daily. Particularly, cathedrals popular with tour groups. But in towns and villages, churches are likely to be locked except during services. And with Protestant churches, God knows—Sunday morn?]

11. Problem: How to walk among mountains without losing your way. Solution: When planning to walk a trail near mountains or "hills" with elevations higher than 1000 ft. (300 m.), copy or buy a topographic map. Or anyway, do not improvise a hike on the spot, among such heights, without carrying *some*

Appendix

kind of map and a compass. (Exception: Where there exists a road up, and a downhill trail off that road near the top, take them.) [Following trails downhill with no map is easier in more ways than one.]

12. Problem: How to avoid losing sleep to the cold up in mountains. Solution: With only a summer-weight sleeping bag, before planning to sleep in a tent at an elevation above 7000 ft. (2,000 m.), find out locally what recent mountain night temperatures were. Do so regardless of the season or the temperature at lower elevation. Then, avoid tenting that high if it averaged under 40°F (5°C). Consider doing a day hike instead. Where there is no one handy to ask or phone who might know mountain temperatures, however, take a pre-dawn reading with your own thermometer while camped below the range. Then subtract 3°F per 1000 ft. (300 m.) up to elevations that a topographic map or trail guidebook gives for your intended campsites. Also, during a likely month for it, scope the slopes for snow. (Exception: Where sleeping in trail lodges is possible.)

13. Problem: How to avoid losing a *second* night's sleep up in mountains. Solution: If the night temperature goes below 40°F (5°C), or 45°F (10°C) inside your tent, do not camp again within 1000 ft. (300 m.) of the cold elevation in that same region. (Exceptions: After hearing a weather forecast of an immediate warming trend. If carrying a heavy enough winter sleeping bag.)

Appendix

14. Problem: How to get a jump on the crowd at big tourist attractions. Solution: Prior to passing the last town before a likely popular trail, park, garden, temple, ruin, etc. which lies out in the country, think up a strategy for crowd-avoidance. First, consider sleeping near the site for an early start, soon after dawn. Sleep in or near entire well-preserved old towns or villages likely to attract tour buses. And avoid weekends or holidays if something else can be done or seen meantime without leaving the area. [For fewer people, less air pollution in cities, and often fewer clouds over the sun in early morning. Fewer eyes helps shy people get their bearings.]

15. Problem: How to avoid a mugging after getting off a city bus in the wrong neighborhood after dark. Solution: On the wrong city bus, after dark, remain on-board through any dangerous-looking neighborhood. Get off only where the city looks well-lit and safe. Ride to the end of the line, if necessary, pay a second fare, and ride back to a safer-looking stop. (Exception: Maybe get off sooner if a waiting taxi is spotted.)

16. Problem: How to stay out of trouble after dark. Solution: (Developing) Stay off beaches after dark. And in general, avoid walking outdoors then, whether in city or country, without good reason.

17. Problem: When to buy a first-class transportation ticket. Solution: (Developing) For long trips on trains or boats, always buy first-class tickets, where available. (Exception: Where a

Appendix

guidebook or experience suggests it is no more difficult to find a comfortable seat in a cheaper class.)

18. Problem: How to find a hotel room in a city overcrowded with visitors. Solution: (Foreign) Arriving in afternoon or later at a city popular with tour groups, during its busy season, or during some kind of big festival, start your hotel search at the tourist office rather than by going directly to guidebook-recommended places. Unless they are quite close to the terminal, try phoning for a reservation rather than walking around.

19. Problem: What to do when your trail seemingly gives out. Solution: When in doubt about the course of a faint trail, stop, look all around, notice what seems to be the path of least resistance onward—look for more trail there. Not finding it, however, return to the last of the clear trail. Look around again there. As a last resort, walk in a wide circle outward and around the trail's farthest clear point, seeking its continuation. [Performing these maneuvers before following an uncertain path steeply downhill is especially advisable.]

20. Problem: How to survive steep off-trail climbs or descents. Solution: In the first place, avoid steep climbs or descents off-trail. Nonetheless, should one be necessary, always give close attention to finding a route well ahead of your position. Thus, before starting to climb steeply uphill, look for a high vantage point facing the slope from which to choose a likely route. Pick out the one with the best foot- and hand-holds. Before, however, climbing either down a steep rocky slope or doing

Appendix

an up-and-back traverse of one, remember that spotting the easiest way past nearly vertical places will be difficult while *descending*. So consider piling or poking in recognizable stones or sticks to mark the best way over extra-steep parts while ascending, if returning by the same path. And if traversing broken mountain terrain, keep to ridges visible from afar—avoid following stream gullies. [Looking down, it is often impossible to see a route all the way, due to rock overhangs. Leaning out to find footholds will likely be necessary. Unlike when walking down a more gradual slope, where path-finding is simpler headed downhill.]

21. Problem: How about a hike or hitchhiking in a disaster or danger area? Solution: Do not walk or hitch within specific areas or on trails said to have bandits, insurgents, unusual dangers, famines, the aftermaths of war, or other big disasters.

22. Problem: How to keep ants out of your gear in areas they swarm. Solution: After noticing a high density of ants, do not leave your pack on the ground in their vicinity for long. Regardless of whether they penetrated your tent the previous night, do not trust them to stay out of gear left either inside or outside it during daylight hours. [The majority of ants in a species may prefer day shift.]

23. Problem: What to do in a developing country when told that all reservations to your destination are booked out. Solution: (Developing) Do not try being wait-listed for a plane seat unless already at the airport. Instead, when told all airlines to

Appendix

your destination are booked out, try a different travel agent. Or else reserve for a different date. (Exceptions: When offered a wait-list number of 5 or below. If some airline representative says that your chance of getting a seat is quite good, consider going long before flight time to the airport and asking once again for a reservation before accepting wait-listing.)

24. Problem: How to have something repaired abroad. Solution: (Foreign) For any sort of necessary repair service, try to find a shop where some English is spoken. Otherwise, find someone to translate your instructions, observations, or questions by phone. [Here is another occasion when being multilingual might really help.]

25. Problem: How to buy a topographic map. Solution: Prior to going for a topographic map at a government agency, have underlined and bookmarked in your trail guidebook the names of the last village before trailhead, the final one at trail's end, and all major geographical features the hike will pass. Also take a roadmap showing where the trailhead nearest your road lies.

26. Problem: How to avoid heat exhaustion and so on. Solution: When perspiring heavily, especially in low humidity, take a salt tablet.

27. Problem: How often and how much should you fill your canteen? Solution: Do not follow a trail uphill from a water source when your canteen is less than half full—stop and fill it. In arid country, stop when less than full. But even in a wet

Appendix

area, fill it completely at any good stream within a mile (2 km.) or so of what may prove to be a dry camp in an otherwise promising map position. (Exceptions: In wet areas, where most streams have several branches, maybe wait a while for a deeper or clearer one to appear. When about to walk through a village or town, get it there from a tap.)

28. Problem: How to spend less time on a hike walking uphill under a full backpack. Solution: For a scenic area less than 20 miles (32 km.) across but with an elevation change of more than 1,000 ft. (300 m.)—such as a desert rock formation, alpine plateau, or canyon—plan no traverse with backpack up or across to its far side. Instead, camp at its base or rim, near water, until early morning. Then day hike up, across, or around it, with only your daypack. (Exception: With some important sight or trail on, in, or over it that may take more than one day to reach or complete.)

29. Problem: How to avoid jock itch. Solution: In hot regions, try to change undershorts daily. Forced to wear either undershorts or socks a second day, though, apply antifungal powder to vulnerable areas and anywhere itching has begun. But escalate to antifungal cream beneath a bandaid for a visible rash, or if itching continues after one day.

30. Problem: What is the easiest way to spot wildlife? Solution: To see wildlife along the shore of a large body of water, frequently stop and sit facing it. Scan offshore rocks, etc. with binoculars. [More wildlife is seen while sitting quietly and

Appendix

watching than while walking. Especially if its likely direction of sighting is known—as when facing a shoreline.]

31. Problem: How to know the best times of day to hike beaches or snorkel. **Solution:** A day or so before starting an isolated beach hike longer than a day, or before snorkeling anywhere, learn the times of low and high tides (which occur 6–7 hours apart). (Modern) Obtain or copy a tide table. (Developing) With no tide table available, ask or observe the tide times. Then try to walk beaches mostly during periods of low tide—especially those said to be impassible in places at high tide and those featuring tide pools. Snorkeling is usually better at low tide, also. (Exception: Where there is something best seen at high tide, such as a blowhole.)

32. Problem: How to avoid drowning in the ocean. **Solution:** No swimming from beaches with strong undertow or strong and unusual currents caused by erratic wave action. When in doubt, don't go far out. [Test: float a buoyant object in the water. If it moves appreciably, that shows a current.]

33. Problem: How to survive on the sea after being captured by a rip current. **Solution:** Pulled out to sea by a rip current, do not try swimming against it. Swim across it. Parallel the shore and then, as its pull weakens, swim toward the beach while angling away from the rip. Furthermore, while doing so, watch ahead to avoid dark paths of calm water (how a rip current looks) or any area behind gaps in the breakers (marking a deep-water channel.) And also try avoiding sea

Appendix

areas of murky brown water, or a choppy and rippled water surface.

34. Problem: How do you decide from whom to buy, where bargaining is customary? Solution: (Developing) Where bargaining is customary, and with a choice of convenient places to buy something, choose the place with the gentlest-looking salesperson. [Rats bargain hardest.]

35. Problem: What to do if, when bargaining, you think you are being overcharged? Solution: (Developing) Buying something inexpensive with no marked price, and intuition suggests that you are being overcharged, offer less than the price asked. Then if the seller holds firm, go elsewhere. [Small gyps are regrettable.]

36. Problem: How to wash off saltwater after an ocean swim. Solution: Soon after ocean swimming, take a shower (soap and shampoo optional). Take even a cold shower. At popular beaches, watch for outdoor showers—often near the swimming pools of waterfront hotels. Or swim a lap in their pool. (Modern) Look for showers in the Harbor Master's building at small boat harbors. [Otherwise, expect to itch and stink.]

37. Problem: When should sunscreen be applied? Solution: Before going out in the sun for more than half an hour, apply sunscreen salve to your lips, and sunscreen lotion to other exposed skin. Do so in the morning every day the sun is out

Appendix

from spring through early autumn in temperate climates and during all seasons in the tropics. Even with a deep tan.

38. Problem: To where should sunscreen lotion be applied before snorkeling? Solution: Before snorkeling, either put on a T-shirt or have someone cover your entire back and shoulders thoroughly with waterproof sunscreen. Also, having worn boots with socks of late, smear it on your ankles down to your flippers or water-shoe tops, and the skin that your wristwatch, etc. covered, too. (Exception: Not to your back and upper arms when already well-tanned.)

39. Problem: What kind of sunscreen lotion to buy. Solution: Buy sunscreen with at least one of the following ingredients: parsol 1789; avobenzone; dioxybenzone; ecamsule; zinc oxide; titanium dioxide. Get SPF 30 or higher—as high as possible. [For pale skin.]

40. Problem: How to identify and take advantage of premonition dreams. Solution: Form the habit of remembering your dreams at the moment of wakening. Then record any seemingly significant one. Decide whether that dream is the type forewarning of a danger or large mistake threatening your future. [Such a dream usually has a memorable emotional charge of sorrow or fear attached, has at least one memorable patch of color in it, is perhaps more obvious in its symbolism than most, and may tend to occur toward morning.]

Finding a dream probably of the premonitory warning type, make an immediate substantial change in your activities

Appendix

planned for the day. Take a different path, or change your itinerary; postpone or cancel risky tasks. Then, if the same or a variation of the same unpleasant dream recurs, imagine to what danger or large mistake in the longer term it probably refers, and consider how to avoid that. [*"There are more things in heaven and earth, Horatio, than are dreamt of in your philosophy."* —Shakespeare]

41. Problem: What extra gear should you maybe rent for snorkeling? Solution: Where available, rent a lifejacket for snorkeling. [They save much energy in staying afloat on waves face down. And wearing one, you can go out farther without anxiety.] Also consider renting a wetsuit before snorkeling when the water temperature is below 70°F (20°C). For water below 60°F (15°C), consider renting accessories to cover feet, head, and hands. [Such low water temperatures outside the tropics are normal, except sometimes in summer.]

42. Problem: How to keep most of the bugs out when camping in jungle. Solution: In jungle, opening your tent's (or hammock's) mosquito netting after dark, even briefly, is to be avoided. As is leaving it unzipped too long during the day. [The nearest ground-dwelling creepy-crawly may pop in for a quick bite. Spiders, ants, and snakes are three reasons why hammocks with mosquito netting are somewhat better than tents for jungle; lighter weight to carry in tropical heat and their coolness are two more.]

43. Problem: When is it best to visit major ruins? Solution: The night before an early-morning visit to major ruins, set your

Appendix

alarm or mental alarm to get up before dawn, if necessary, to arrive the moment they open. Especially famous ones, and those near big cities or resorts. [Too many people scare away ghosts.]

44. Problem: How to decide between a bus and a van. Solution: Where both buses and vans are available to some destination more than 10 miles (16 km.) distant, choose a bus. (Exception: If waiting time for a bus is over an hour extra.) [Buses are likely to have more comfortable seats, higher windows for more view, lower cost, and more safety in an accident.]

45. Problem: How to walk a short distance in jungle without getting lost. Solution: When a jungle trail is blocked by an obstacle so large that a detour around it is necessary—usually, one or several fallen trees with their vines—look for a fainter semi-circular trail to the side. And then, while on it, or while making one, stay focused on the fact of your being off the main trail by consciously repeating your present relation to the obstacle. Think over and over: "Thing to my left (right)," etc. [Walking a faint trail in jungle for even a short distance risks losing your way while daydreaming.]

46. Problem: How to walk a longer distance in jungle without getting lost. Solution: Going off-trail in jungle more than about 5 paces for any reason, perhaps in looking for a campsite, note the compass direction to return. Then count your paces away from the trail, while trying to walk mostly in a straight line. (Exception: Following a watercourse, counting paces is

Appendix

unnecessary; just remember to keep its sound always on your left or right side.)

47. Problem: How to remember compass bearings. Solution: To help remember a compass bearing, visualize a map of your country as a compass face. Then commit to memory the name of a region, state, or province in it corresponding to your compass bearing. For instance, using a USA map outline as a diagram, think "New England" to remember a N.E. bearing, or "Arizona" to remember S.W., or "Minnesota" for North, and so on. [After taking a compass reading, it's easier to visualize and remember a place-named map image than to remember either letters ("S.W.") or a directional word ("southwest").]

48. Problem: How to cross or avoid army-ant or termite columns. Solution: Occasionally in a jungle, a column of army ants too wide to step over may carpet your trail. Stride or run through them fast. Then, on the far side, stamp your boots hard as if knocking off snow. After that, pick off one-by-one all those still climbing your legs. Also, mainly in the tropics, watch the ground and tree trunks to avoid even single-file columns of ants or termites when choosing a tent or hammock site.

49. Problem: How far to put up with backpacking on pavement where any mode of transportation is possible. Solution: With a full pack, to go more than 2 miles (3 km.) on a paved road, ride a public conveyance, or hitch. Even on downhill pavement through good scenery. For a shorter distance, either hike or hitch/hike, depending upon scenery and slope. [Backpacking on pavement is hard on feet and legs, and risks still harder contact with passing automobiles.]

50. Problem: How to decide whether to do your own laundry in a hotel sink. Solution: (Foreign) In a city with no self-service laundry, in a country where haggling over hotel rates is unusual, ask if someone employed by the hotel does laundry. If not, ask for directions to a nearby laundry shop. However, in a country where haggling over hotel rates prevails, do your own. Also do your own in some particular developing country or city where laundry service is unusually expensive. (Exceptions: When it is rainy or overcast on your washday in a haggling country, then ask at a nearby store, not your hotel, for the nearest laundry. Or, if a hotel in a haggling country has laundry rates posted on a sign, use its service.) [In some countries, doing your own laundry is quicker and easier than finding someone else to do it and then haggling the cost.]

About the Author

Over the past fifty years, Charles Bowden has traveled extensively throughout North America, Latin America, Asia, Australia, North Africa, Europe, and the Middle East. One of the most insightful travel writers of our time, he is the author of *Zeke's Guide to Travel & Life*, a multi-volume series on his shared explorations with Zeke—his travel companion and the focus of his work as a biographer. Bowden's one-of-a-kind travel guides are filled with honest and humorous perceptions, travel tips, and critical reviews of some of the world's most sightly, must-see locales. His thought-provoking narratives stem from unabated curiosity about the world, its natural beauty, and the people who inhabit its distant lands.

www.ingramcontent.com/pod-product-compliance
Lightning Source LLC
Chambersburg PA
CBHW021058080526
44587CB00010B/294